GOLD AND THE GOLD STANDARD

GOLD AND THE GOLD STANDARD

The Story of Gold Money
Past, Present and Future

BY

EDWIN WALTER KEMMERER

Emeritus Professor of International Finance
Princeton University

FIRST EDITION
SECOND IMPRESSION

McGRAW-HILL BOOK COMPANY, Inc.
NEW YORK AND LONDON
1944

Prefatory Note

At the end of the war, this world will be confronted with the problem of rehabilitating its monetary systems and of thereby bringing order out of the monetary chaos that has been created. Many different kinds of monetary standards will have their advocates, and the debate will be a vigorous one in terms of both light and heat. Early discussions of the problem should contribute to the formation of an intelligent public opinion. It is with the thought of making such a contribution that this book is being written.

Prominent among the contenders for first position in the world's monetary systems of the early postwar future will be the gold standard, which, though badly battered and bruised, can still claim, by reason of its past record, to be the heir apparent.

The discussion that follows attempts to explain briefly the origin and history of gold money and of the gold standard, the fundamental principles of the gold standard, its defects and merits, and to outline a plan for a future international gold standard.

In the preparation of this book I have received aid from many friends—too many to mention by name in a brief prefatory note. I must, however, make

[v]

exception by expressing my particular gratitude to Dr. Louis C. West and Professor Philip K. Hitti, of Princeton, for their valuable suggestions concerning the money of ancient times, and to my son Professor Donald L. Kemmerer, of the University of Illinois, and Professor Oskar Morgenstern, of Princeton, both of whom read the entire manuscript and gave me many useful criticisms and suggestions, most of which I have adopted.

EDWIN WALTER KEMMERER.

PRINCETON, N. J.,
October, 1944.

Contents

[vii]

CONTENTS

CONTENTS

CHAPTER VI

CHAPTER VII

CHAPTER VIII

[ix]

Gold and the Gold Standard

CHAPTER I

The Place of Gold in the Money of Ancient and Medieval Times

Speak of the moderns without contempt and of the ancients without idolatry; judge them all by their merits and not by their age.—LORD CHESTERFIELD, 1748.

ORIGIN OF THE GOLD STANDARD

The gold standard in its "orthodox form" is a product of the nineteenth century. Its roots, however, go deep into the past. This chapter will explore briefly this early history of gold as money,[1] *i.e.*, as a commonly accepted medium of exchange.

Gold, by reason of its beauty, its world-wide distribution, the facility with which it could be obtained from the streams by crude methods of "panning," and the ease with which it could be "worked," probably had a wider use as a medium of exchange in very ancient times,[2] and among primitive peoples in modern times, than any other metal.

This metal was first used as money in such forms as nuggets of gold, gold molded in the shape of

[1] For a brief discussion of the origin, nature, and definition of money, see Edwin Walter Kemmerer, *Money*, pp. 3–16.

[2] *Cf.* RIDGEWAY, WILLIAM, *The Origin of Metallic Currency and Weight Standards*, pp. 57–58.

[3]

shells, which served also as ornaments, and gold dust. In ancient Mexico, Africa, and elsewhere, gold was put into transparent quills, which were used as a common means of payment. It circulated in small cubes in China as early as 1100 B.C. Many hundreds of years before the beginning of the Christian Era, gold media of exchange were used in Asia Minor and a large part of Europe. These early media were usually made of almost pure gold, the art of hardening the metal by means of alloy apparently not having been introduced until after the beginning of the Christian Era.

The earliest references I have been able to find in recorded history to the use of one of the precious metals as a medium of exchange—in these cases, passing by weight—are in the Code of Hammurabi,[1] King of Babylon. They refer to silver in about the year 1870 B.C.[2]

The peoples of classical times had very little knowledge of the money of their early ancestors. They had no books on money, and the few written records available to them were chiefly on stone and papyri in the form of laws, decrees, and scattered miscellaneous notes. By far the most important

---

[1] "If a man have destroyed the eye of a freedman, or have broken the bone of a freedman, he shall pay one mina of silver" (§198). "If a doctor have operated . . . he shall receive ten shekels of silver" (§215). "The wage of an artisan . . . five Sĕ of silver, of a brickmaker . . . five Sĕ. . . . " (§274).

[2] Like the names of many other monetary units of later times (*i.e.*, pound, peso, lira), the mina and the shekel were originally concepts of weight. The mina was an ancient Babylonian unit of weight, and shekel (Hebrew, *shegal*) meant "to weigh" and equaled $\frac{1}{60}$ of a mina.

part of our records of these early times consists of the money itself, which has been preserved and is now held largely in the museums of the world, where it is classified and catalogued. The coined money alone of classical times that has been thus preserved runs into tens of thousands of pieces; and the weights of these pieces, the materials of which the coins are made, their forms, and especially the designs and legends that they bear give us valuable information.

Thanks to the careful studies made by classical scholars over many generations, we know today much more about the money of classical times than the ancients knew. There are, however, many gaps in the chronology of the coins that have come down to us, and the story that these coins tell is far from complete. It is still full of controversial questions concerning which the modern literature is voluminous, but progress in their solution is being made continually.[1]

EARLY COINAGE IN ASIA MINOR

Coinage was originally of the nature of a seal or hallmark punched on a nugget of metal as a guarantee of its quality or its weight. The beginnings of coinage appear to have been made in the countries of the

---

[1] Obviously, it is impracticable in a book such as this to do more than to touch briefly on the more elementary facts and principles. Where important controversial questions are involved, the best we can do is to follow a highly responsible recent authority and to refer the reader to the selected bibliography at the end of the chapter, in which a number of the principal studies (some of them containing extensive bibliographies) are cited.

[5]

eastern Mediterranean early in the eighth century B.C.[1] Sennacherib, King of Assyria (705–681 B.C.), said, "I built a form of clay and poured bronze into it as in making half-shekel pieces."

Many of the early coins were made of electrum—a natural alloy, consisting of about three parts of gold to one part of silver, which was found abundantly in Lydia and which caused that country to be known as *the land of gold*. Because of the difficulty in separating the gold from the silver, the ancients regarded electrum almost as a distinct metal. Early coins of pure gold in Asia Minor were probably made from placer gold obtained from the valley of the Oxus or from the Ural Mountains.[2] The electrum coins were ancient examples of what in modern times is called *symmetallism*.

I have in my possession a gold daric, one of the oldest and most famous gold coins in history. It is made of almost pure gold and is about the weight of our late American $5 gold piece. It looks like a roughly molded gold nugget and bears a crude stamp of an archer with his bow and spear. The coin was made during the reign of Darius the Great of Persia, about 500 years before Christ. Only about two generations before this, in the reign of Croesus, which began 561 B.C., there circulated in Asia Minor the coins of which Herodotus said, "The Lydians were

[1] DUBBERSTEIN, W. H., Comparative Prices in Later Babylonia, *American Journal of Semitic Languages and Literatures*, January, 1939, pp. 20*ff.*

[2] RIDGEWAY, *op. cit.*, pp. 204–205.

the first people, so far as I know, to adopt a gold and silver coinage."[1]

In those early times, gold coins and silver coins circulated for several centuries under a dual standard. Gold gained in importance at the time of Alexander the Great, under the stimulus furnished by the large amount of gold produced in his Pangean mines.[2]

COINAGE IN THE LAND OF THE GREEKS

In Homeric times values in Greece were reckoned in terms of the cow. According to Ridgeway, ". . . weighing was first invented for traffic in gold, and since the weight-unit of gold is found regularly to be the value of a cow or ox . . . the unit of weight is ultimately derived from the value in gold of a cow."[3] Our English word *pecuniary*, which is derived from the Latin *pecus*, meaning "cattle," is a monument to this development. Copper was early used as money. The first obol was apparently a copper spike or skewer, six of which made a drachma, meaning "handful."[4]

The first gold coin to circulate in Hellas proper was the aforementioned Persian daric or stater (meaning "to weigh"), which weighed about 130

[1] Pictures of a number of these very early coins, including one of a gold coin of Croesus, are given by William Atherton DuPuy in The Geography of Money, *The National Geographic Magazine*, December, 1927, pp. 744–768.

[2] BURNS, A. R., *Money and Monetary Policy in Early Times*, p. 157.

[3] For an interesting discussion of the cow unit in different countries and its influence in determining coined units of value, ancient and modern, see Ridgeway, *op. cit.*, pp. 112–115 and 124–154.

[4] CARLILE, WILLIAM WARRAND, *The Evolution of Modern Money*, p. 31.

grains and which enjoyed an extensive circulation for several centuries. It was never debased and was "practically the only gold coin for about 200 years, as well in Asia Minor and the mainland of Greece as in the Persian Empire."[1] It was known in Palestine during Biblical times.

The Greeks learned the use of gold coin from the Asiatics, but they were slow to coin gold themselves. The first place in Hellas proper to mint money was Aegina, which was a commercial center. The silver coins of this small island and the Persian gold darics circulated extensively in Magna Graecia. Solon is believed to have been the first person to coin silver money in Athens. Coins of silver and gold apparently passed at approximately their respective bullion values. In this dual-standard system, silver coins were those most widely used, but gold coins played an extensive part in the country's foreign trade, also in many of the larger domestic transactions and for reserves in the temples. In times of war and other great emergencies, there was an increased coinage of gold from metal obtained by melting down golden statues and ornaments, which were obtained largely from the temples.

Early in the fourth century B.C., the silver coinage of Rhodes was supplemented by an issue of gold staters, and this double issue of gold and silver continued unbroken[2] until after the death of Alexander the Great in 323 B.C.

[1] Burns, *op. cit.*, p. 160.
[2] Ridgeway, *op. cit.*, p. 339.

In the Greek world there were, on occasions, official ratings of the coins of one metal in terms of those of the others. Ratings were changed from time to time and recoinages were made, to prevent a cheaper or overrated metal from driving out of circulation a dearer or underrated one, under the force of what we now call Gresham's law.[1]

About the beginning of the fourth century B.C., we find a case of monetary debasement suggestive of our American debasement of 1933 to 1934.[2] Dionysius, Tyrant of Syracuse, who had borrowed heavily from his citizens and was being hard pressed for repayment, directed that all the coins in the city should be brought to him, under penalty of death. He then restamped the coins and gave to each drachma the value of two drachmas. By this debasement he was enabled to pay off the original loan and, at the same time, repay the money that he had ordered to be brought to the mint.[3]

Shortly after the death of Alexander, the unified Attic monetary system, which prevailed throughout most of his empire, began to disintegrate. Concerning what followed, down to the time of the conquest of the Greek world by the Romans, M. Rostovtzeef says:[4]

---

[1] The principle of Gresham's law appears to have been known in ancient Greece. Aristophanes, writing about 405 B.C., said in *Frogs*, "In our Republic bad citizens are preferred to good. Just as bad money circulates while good money disappears." For a brief explanation of Gresham's law, see pp. 135–136, note.

[2] *Cf.* pp. 128–130.

[3] BULLOCK, CHARLES JESSE, *Economic Essays*, p. 508.

[4] ROSTOVTZEEF, M., *The Social and Economic History of the Hellenistic World*, p. 1291.

[Alexander's] successors continued his coinage but each for himself in his own name: Coinage was one of the signs and symbols of political independence, it was a powerful instrument of political influence and propaganda, and it yielded a substantial revenue. With the further disintegration of his empire, coinage became ever more diversified, each sovereign State, whether a monarchy or a city, minting its own money.

THE POSITION OF GOLD IN THE MONEY OF ANCIENT ROME

Gold played a much less important role in the money of Italian lands in early historic times than it did in Asia Minor and in Greece. Nonetheless, in the form of ingots and of foreign coins, it was used there as money to some extent as early as the fourth century B.C. Some gold coins were struck in the year 206 B.C., at the time of the Second Punic War. By the fourth century A.D., there was a preference for gold over silver and by the seventh century the preference for gold was well established. Accounts were often kept in terms of gold, even when payments had to be made in silver or bronze. The following brief history of money during classical times among the Romans will show the place of gold.

Bronze Money. In Italy, as elsewhere, one of the first forms of metallic money consisted of unstamped bullion. But here, unlike the situation in some other places, where gold was readily available, the first metal to circulate was bronze. Originally, the bronze circulated in the form of a rough lump (*aes rude*), the lumps varying in weight, shape, and size, and bearing no stamp. Later it was hammered into the form of a bar, known as an *as*[1] (meaning "unit") in order to give it a convenient form for bartering the metal, which was in demand for the making of tools, weapons, and utensils. As time went on, the conventional length of this bar became a foot (the length of a man's foot), which, with the conventional diameter, gave the bar a convenient weight of about 1 pound.[2] The bar was later marked off into 12 thumbs, or inches. Since these bars (*asses*) varied considerably in weight, the custom gradually developed of passing them by weight instead of by tale. The weight of metal then became the important consideration, and the unit of value became the pound of bronze, the *as libralis*, while the 12 thumb divisions, or inches, became 12 ounces.[3]

Summing up this development, Ridgeway says:[4]

There is no positive evidence to show that the original monetary *as* was a foot long, but, as the *as-pes*, it is certain that the *as* was originally a piece of copper a foot in length and of a known thickness. As soon as the rods or *asses* were exchanged by weighing, they began to lose their original form, which was only essential so long as it was necessary that they should be of certain fixed dimensions. Under the new system

[1] The history of the Roman as is both intriguing and controversial. Concerning it there is a voluminous literature.

[2] The Roman pound contained 12 ounces and the ounce was divided into 24 scruples. It is usually equated with 5,057 grains Troy. See Louis C. West, Gold and Silver Coin Standards in the Roman Empire, *Numismatic Notes and Monographs*, No. 4 (1941), pp. 6 and 34.

[3] RIDGEWAY, in Sir John Edwin Sandys's *A Companion to Latin Studies*, p. 441.

[4] *Ibid.*, p. 447.

the shape mattered not, provided the *as* was of full weight when placed in the scale.

Weighing bronze was, however, inconvenient, and the practice developed toward the close of the regal period of placing upon the asses an authoritative stamp certifying their weight, so that again they could pass by count. There are early records of 2-pound bars and also of bars of ½ and ¼ pound. The earliest coin marks on the bars that we have preserved are crude drawings of animals. According to Pliny,[1] "King Servius first stamped bronze. . . . It was stamped with the impressions of animals, whence it was termed *pecunia* . . . "

The as of bronze, which developed as a commodity-money unit of value very early in Roman history and was first coined about 300 B.C., played an important part in that history for centuries. According to Mattingly, "The bronze coinage was paramount from the beginnings down to *c.* 245 B.C. . . . " While from 245 B.C. to 217 B.C. it played an equally important part with silver,[2] after 217 B.C. silver dominated, and during the second century the bronze coinage became increasingly subsidiary.

During its early history, the coined as (with its divisions and multiples) was a commodity-money unit, *i.e.*, it circulated at its bullion value of 1 pound of bronze, and was known as the *as libralis*. It was the standard unit of value. As standard money, it

---

[1] Gaius Plinius Secundus, *Historia Naturalis*, Bk. XXXIII, 3.13.
[2] Mattingly, Harold, *Roman Coins*, pp. 18 and 27.

suffered several debasements. During the First Punic War, according to Pliny, the weight of the as was reduced, "when the republic, being unable to defray its expenses, resolved to coin six *asses* out of the pound; whereby they gained five parts, and paid their debts." Before the end of the Second Punic War, the as had been debased again by 50 per cent, thereby reaching a weight of 1 ounce, the *as uncial*. Somewhat later, the as coins became token money, subsidiary to silver. As such, their weights were further reduced from time to time, but since they were mere token coins, these reductions probably did not materially affect their money value.

Long after the *as libralis* ceased to circulate, it was used as a unit of account, in terms of which people thought and expressed monetary values even when payments were actually made in the standard silver money.[1] In contracts then it appears to have been called the *as grave*, to distinguish it from the current as.

History has given us a descendant of the word *as* (unit) in our word *ace* and descendants of the word *aes* (bronze), as used in *aes rude* (p. 10), in our words *esteem* and *estimate*.

Silver Money. Silver in the form of ingots and of foreign coins, notably those of the Greeks, Etruscans, and Sicilians, circulated in Italy during part

---

[1] It is interesting to note that our word *money* has its origin in early Roman times. Money then was coined in a temple of Juno on Capitoline Hill in Rome. One of Juno's many names was Moneta, a word cognate with Latin *monere* (to warn). Moneta was guardian of finances (as well as the protector of the female sex). Our words *money* and *mint* are cognate with Moneta.

of the bronze-standard period just described. According to Mattingly,[1] the *aes grave* of Rome and Italy, which we have previously mentioned, represented "only a short stage of transition from the early use of uncoined bronze as a measure of value, to the Greek use of silver money . . . " Rome, learning the use of silver and of token bronze from the Greeks of southern Italy, was led to give at least the form of a coinage to the bronze that she was accustomed to use for trading with the Italian peoples.

It was inevitable that this clumsy coinage should soon give way to the more convenient silver. Accordingly, during the course of the Pyrrhic War, Rome struck her first silver coins, didrachmas (double drachmas) and rare divisions of the didrachma.[2] After defeating Pyrrhus and getting control of all southern Italy, shortly before the First Punic War, the Romans obtained there large supplies of silver, which they used in part for the Roman silver coin that was struck in Campania. This coin was the denarius (meaning "every ten"), and was probably equivalent to a didrachma. It was rated at 10 asses and divided into four parts, called *sestertii*. Although this silver coinage in Rome itself was struck about 268 B.C., it was not until about a half century later that silver became the dominant standard and the sestertius replaced the as as the unit of reckoning.[3]

[1] MATTINGLY, HAROLD, The First Age of Roman Coinage, *Journal of Roman Studies*, Vol. 19, pp. 20 and 23.

[2] MATTINGLY, *Roman Coins*, pp. 5–6.

[3] *Ibid.*, p. 24.

In the year 217 B.C. the as was reduced to a standard of 1 ounce and was retariffed at the rate of 16 instead of 10 to the denarius, while the denarius itself was debased. About the beginning of the second century B.C., "the Roman coinage enters on a long period of quiet and orderly movement with little of external change to mark it."[1] This situation continued during the early centuries of the Empire,[2] during which, however, silver met increasing competition from gold. The yellow metal finally superseded silver as the dominant standard, just as silver had previously superseded bronze. To this story we shall now turn.

GOLD MONEY DURING THE REPUBLIC

Contemporaneously with the circulation of bronze and silver in Rome and other Italian cities during early times, there was a circulation by weight of gold in the form of nuggets and of foreign coins. This gold was used principally in the larger transactions. Although destined ultimately to supplant both bronze and silver as the basic monetary metal, gold was in this territory the least important of the three, prior to the beginning of the Christian Era. Evidence that there was a substantial circulation of

[1] *Ibid.*, p. 17.

[2] Silver was the principal money of Palestine during the early years of the Christian Era. Gold and bronze coins, however, also circulated there. Christ, for example, directed the twelve disciples, "Provide neither gold, nor silver, nor brass in your purses" (Matt. 10:9). The Greek word for silver is the word translated "money" in the passage "For the love of money is the root of all evil" (I Tim. 6:10). All the references to money that occur in the New Testament have been gathered together by West, *op. cit.*, pp. 47–48.

gold as early as the fourth century B.C. is found in the fact that there was a law at that time requiring that a certain tax be paid in gold.[1]

Under the financial strain of the Second Punic War (218–201 B.C.), Rome for the first time minted gold coins. They were minted out of gold bullion taken from her treasury.[2] The weights of these coins were based on the scruple,[3] which was one twenty-fourth of the old Roman ounce and equaled 17½ grains. There were coins, of one, two, and three scruples, respectively, with the approximate weights that would correspond to $1, $2, and $3 of United States gold coin prior to 1933. The Romans officially rated these gold pieces in terms of silver at a rate of 20 sestertii to a scruple of gold, a rating so high that apparently the gold coins were treated as tokens. The issue was short-lived.[4]

No further gold coins were minted by Rome for over a century and a half, until the time of the Roman conquests under the great generals Sulla, Pompey, and Julius Caesar. These generals in the field issued the gold coins under authority of the government at Rome. Much of the metal for making them came to the generals in the form of loot, and

---

[1] Burns, *op. cit.*, p. 151.

[2] *Ibid.;* also, Mattingly, *Roman Coins*, pp. 14 and 24.

[3] Raper, Matthew, An Inquiry into the Value of the Ancient Greek and Roman Money, in J. R. McCulloch's *Old and Scarce Tracts on Money*, p. 552.

The word *scruple* seems to have been developed from the etymological sense "small pebble."

[4] Mattingly, *Roman Coins*, pp. 151–152.

many of the coins in turn probably went to the soldiers as rewards. Sulla coined an aureus (meaning gold) of 168 grains and later one of 140 grains. Pompey continued coining it at 140 grains. Julius Caesar reduced it to 126 grains.[1] After his death the Senate authorized the ordinary moneyers to coin gold, but coining at Rome was soon superseded by the provincial issues of the triumvirs and their subordinates.[2]

When, as a result of debasements, coins of different weights were in circulation together in sufficient quantities, Gresham's law operated, and the lighter weight coins drove the heavier ones out of circulation. A person who could discharge a debt with the same number of lightweight aurei as of heavyweight ones, naturally paid it with the lightweight ones and kept or melted down the heavier ones. Likewise, when the market prices of commodities were the same whether payments were made in lightweight coins or in heavyweight ones, the purchaser would pay with the lightweight ones. It was merely a case of buying in the cheaper market. To the extent that the merchants and others in selling goods made allowance for the differences in the weight of the coins by quoting lower prices when payment was to be made in the heavier coins, a dual standard developed and

[1] These gold coins were probably not rated as so many silver denarii, but were bought and sold at market prices. "The aureus of Julius Caesar of ¼ pound . . . is the direct predecessor of the imperial aureus of Augustus, which was tariffed at 25 denarii."—MATTINGLY, *Roman Coins*, p. 25.

[2] *Ibid.*, p. 18.

standard coins of different weights then circulated side by side.[1]

GOLD MONEY DURING THE EMPIRE IN THE WEST

With the extensive coining of gold by the generals during the later years of the Republic, gold coins came to stay for a long time, although during the following centuries they had many vicissitudes.

Augustus gave gold a place above silver.[2] He reduced the aureus from the 126-grains weight given it by Julius Caesar to 122.9 grains. "Gold and silver are both struck almost pure [at a ratio of 12½ to 1]. . . . Brass and copper are struck much more carelessly . . . , *i.e.*, not on a carefully adjusted weight for each piece, but at so many to the pound."[3] From Augustus to Nero the system was not changed, but the weight of the aureus was gradually reduced administratively, with an accompanyng reduction in the denarius. From the reign of Nero through the reign of Diocletian, the monetary situation throughout the Empire was confused and debasements were common. The reigns of Claudius and Nero witnessed much counterfeiting and a wide circulation of privately made tokens, which were usually of lead.[4]

---

[1] *Cf.* pp. 135–136, and KEMMERER, *Modern Currency Reforms*, pp. 329–330.

[2] MATTINGLY, *Roman Coins*, pp. 18 and 123.

[3] *Ibid.*, p. 123. The aureus and the silver denarius, with their respective divisions, were tariffed as follows: 1 aureus (122.9 gr.) = 25 denarii = 100 sestertii = 400 asses. 1 denarius (61.46 gr.) = 4 sestertii = 16 asses.

[4] ROSTOVTZEEF, M., *The Social and Economic History of the Roman Empire*, pp. 171–172.

Diocletian made two reductions in the weight of the aureus in the year 312, and Constantine the Great put through a monetary reform that fixed the gold content of the aureus at about 70 grains, representing a debasement of approximately 38 per cent since the time of Nero. Thereafter, until the Empire in the West came to its end in 476, gold apparently grew in relative importance[1] and was the imperial money par excellence, although the silver denarius and its fractions continued to hold a high place in the business of the Empire.[2]

The Place of Gold in the Money of Continental Europe during the Middle Ages

An elementary historical study of gold in the money of the Middle Ages can be brief, because the records that have come down to us for this period are meager and are not of great significance to the student of monetary science.

Characteristics of the Economy of the Middle Ages

There were three important factors influencing the monetary history of the Middle Ages. The first of these factors was the development of the feudal system, with its large landed estates, its practice of subinfeudation and hierarchy of authority from the overlords down through the various grades of vassals to the serfs and slaves, and with its payments

[1] BURNS, op. cit., p. 154.
[2] WEST, op. cit., p. 6.

[19]

in kind and in personal services. All this made the great manorial estates largely self-sufficient economically. They produced most of what they consumed and consumed most of what they produced. The volume of trade, therefore, relative to the population, was much smaller than it had been in classical times.

The second factor was the circumstance that much of the small amount of trade that did take place was carried on by means of simple barter. Money was unnecessary.

The third factor was that the supply of the precious metals available for money declined in a large part of Europe during the Dark Ages. Widespread looting of occupied territories during the wars of the early Christian Era and subsequently by the conquering Germanic peoples of the North had scattered widely and thinly the accumulated gold and silver treasure of classical times. The yields of the gold and silver mines also declined, partly because the mines were bled white by tenant operators who were little concerned with the conservation of the mines' resources, partly because most of the labor in the mines was inefficient convict and slave labor, and partly because there was destruction and looting of the mines by the invading barbarians.[1]

---

[1] JACOBS, WILLIAM, *An Historical Inquiry into the Production and Consumption of the Precious Metals*, vol. I. See, also, WALKER, FRANCIS A., *International Bimetallism*, pp. 16–24.

Coinage in Europe during the early Middle Ages was practically limited to silver and copper, except for a temporary minting of gold in the Carolingian period. Silver provided the principal currency of western Europe. The aureus of Constantine, however, continued to circulate until the downfall of the Eastern Empire in 1453, and from this gold unit various coinages of mediaeval and modern Europe were descended.[1]

Gold Coins

In the year 1252, in response to a growing demand for coins of a larger value, particularly for the foreign trade of the great Italian cities, gold coins containing 48 grains of fine gold were struck in Florence. These became the famous gold florins of Italy.[2] Similar gold coins were later minted in Germany and France, and in other cities of Italy—notably, the Venetian zecchino, which had a large circulation extending even to Turkey.

Gold florins issued in the Italian cities were given official ratings with the silver coins then in circulation. The official rating and the market ratio of gold and silver were frequently at variance, with the usual result that coins of the overvalued metal drove from circulation coins of the undervalued one.

[1] See p. 29, note; also, RIDGEWAY, in Sandys, *op. cit.*, pp. 451–452.
[2] The Italian name was *fiorino*, meaning "flower." The coin had a lily on one side and on the other the Latin name of the city, Florentia.

Seigniorage

Under the feudal system, the prerogative of coining money was exercised by the suzerain or by persons to whom he gave it as a feudal grant. These grants were so extensively given that by the beginning of the ninth century coinage was greatly decentralized in a large part of Europe. The lords of the manor (or *seigneurs,* as they were called in France) were privileged to extract from the gold and silver brought to them for coinage a small percentage to cover the expenses of coinage and to compensate them for their work. This percentage, which was supposed to represent the difference between the value of the bullion in the coin and the value of the coin itself, was called *seigniorage.* The seigneurs, however, developed the practice of extracting from the coin unduly large amounts as seigniorage profits, and during the Middle Ages this was an important cause of currency debasement.

SELECTED BIBLIOGRAPHY

BULLOCK, CHARLES JESSE: *Economic Essays,* Harvard University Press, Cambridge, Mass., 1936.

BURNS, A. R.: *Money and Monetary Policy in Early Times* (with Bibliography), Alfred A. Knopf, New York, 1927.

CARLILE, WILLIAM WARRAND: *The Evolution of Modern Money,* Macmillan & Company, Ltd., London, 1901.

DUBBERSTEIN, W. H.: Comparative Prices in Later Babylonia, *American Journal of Semitic Languages and Literature,* January, 1939.

Du Puy, William Atherton: The Geography of Money, with 31 illustrations, *The National Geographic Magazine*, December, 1927, pp. 744–768.

Finlay, George: A History of Greece. Oxford, Clarendon Press, 1877.

Grueber, H. A.: *Coins of the Roman Republic in the British Museum*, British Museum, London, 1910.

Haeberlin, E. J.: Die Systematik des ältesten römischen Münzwesen, *Verlag der Berliner Münzblätter*, Berlin, 1905.

————: *Aes grave*, 2 vols., J. Baer, Frankfurt a./M., 1910.

Kemmerer, Edwin Walter: *Money*, The Macmillan Company, New York, 1935.

Lexis, W.: Das Münzwesen der neuren Zeit (with Bibliography), *Handwörterbuch der Staatswissenschaften*, Dritte Auflage, 1910, VI, 847–853.

McCulloch, J. R., Editor: *Old and Scarce Tracts on Money*, P. S. King & Son, Ltd., London, 1933.

Mattingly, Harold: *Roman Coins from the Earliest Times to the Fall of the Western Empire*, Methuen & Co., Ltd., London, 1928.

————: *Coins of the Roman Empire in the British Museum*, British Museum, London, 1923

————: *A Guide to the Exhibition of Roman Coins in the British Museum*, British Museum, London, 1927.

————: The First Age of Roman Coinage, *Journal of Roman Studies*, vol. 19, 1929.

Meyer, Edward: Orientalisches und griechisches Münzwesen (with Bibliography), *Handwörterbuch der Staatswissenschaften*, Dritte Auflage, 1910, VI, 824–832.

Mickwitz, Gunnar: *Geld und Wirtschaft im römischen Reich des vierten Jahrhunderts n. Chr.*, Centraltryckeri och Bokbinderi Aktiebolag, Helsingfors, 1932.

Mommsen, Theodor: *Geschichte des römischen Münzwesens*, Weidmannsche Buchhandlung, Berlin, 1860.

————: *Histoire de la monnaie romaine*, translated by de Blacas, 4 vols., Rollin et Feuardent, Paris, 1865–1875.

MORSE, H. B.: *The Trade and Administration of China*, Longmans, Green and Company, New York, 1913.

PICK, B. Römisches Münzwesen (with Bibliography), *Handwörterbuch der Staatswissenschaften*, Dritte Auflage, 1910, VI, 832–839.

RAPER, MATTHEW: An Inquiry into the Value of the Ancient Greek and Roman Money, *Philosophical Transactions*, 1771, reprinted in J. R. McCulloch, *Old and Scarce Tracts on Money*, P. S. King & Son, Ltd., London, 1938.

RIDGEWAY, WILLIAM: *The Origin of Metallic Currency and Weight Standards*, University Press (John Wilson & Son, Inc.), Cambridge, Mass., 1892.

————: Measures and Weights; Money, in Leonard Whibley, *A Companion to Greek Studies*, University Press (John Wilson & Son, Inc.), Cambridge, Mass., 1905.

————: Measures and Weights; Money, in Sir John Edwin Sandys, *A Companion to Latin Studies*, University Press (John Wilson & Son, Inc.), Cambridge, Mass., 1910.

ROSTOVTZEEF, M.: *The Social and Economic History of the Hellenistic World*, 3 vols., Clarendon Press, Oxford University Press, New York, 1941.

————: *The Social and Economic History of the Roman Empire*, Clarendon Press, Oxford University Press, New York, 1926.

SAMWER, K.: *Geschichte des älteren römischen Münzwesens bis ca. 200 v. Chr.*, Berlin, 1883.

SANDYS, SIR JOHN EDWIN: *A Companion to Latin Studies*, University Press (John Wilson & Son, Inc.), Cambridge, Mass., 1910.

SMITH, ADAM: *An Inquiry into the Nature and Causes of the Wealth of Nations*, 2 vols., George Bell & Sons, Ltd., London, 1896.

SOMMERLAD, THEODORE: Mittelalterliches Münzwesen, *Hand-wörterbuch der Staatswissenschaften*, Dritte Auflage, 1910, VI, 839–847.

VISSERING, W. *On Chinese Currency*, E. J. Bell, Leiden, 1877.

WAGEL, SRINIVAS R.: Finance in China, *North-China Daily News & Herald*, Shanghai, 1914.

WALKER, FRANCIS A.: *International Bimetallism*, Henry Holt and Company, Inc., New York, 1897.

WEST, LOUIS C.: Gold and Silver Coin Standards in the Roman Empire (with Bibliography), *Numismatic Notes and Monographs*, No. 4, The American Numismatic Society, New York, 1941.

———: Roman Gold Standard and the Ancient Sources, *American Journal of Philology*, vol. LXII (1941).

WHIBLEY, LEONARD: *A Companion to Greek Studies*, University Press (John Wilson & Son, Inc.), Cambridge, Mass., 1905.

CHAPTER II

Two Thousand Years of Gold Money in England

The English always manage to muddle through.—AUTHOR UNKNOWN, 1885.

England has had more experience with gold as standard money than has any other nation in the world, as well as a longer experience with gold monometallism. This chapter will explore briefly that experience down to 1821, when England's monometallic gold standard came fully into operation.

Chronologically, this history of gold money in England may be divided conveniently into two periods: (1) from ancient times to the discovery of America, and (2) from that date, 1492, to 1821.

DEVELOPMENTS FROM ANCIENT TIMES TO 1492

Gold in the form of bullion and of foreign coins circulated in ancient Britain, along with silver and bronze.

The Britons made their first gold coins about 150 B.C., "taking for their model the coins then current in Gaul, which were themselves copied from those of Philip of Macedon."[1] Coins of gold, silver,

---

[1] KENYON, ROBERT LLOYD, *The Gold Coins of England*, p. 1.

and copper have been found in England, of a character that "cannot have been constructed upon any model introduced subsequent to the establishment of the Romans in Britain."[1] The coins were Greek in origin, but apparently were struck in England. The probable explanation is that "either from commercial visits of the Phoenicians, or through the communications which must have taken place between Britain and Gaul, Grecian coins became known in the Island and were coarsely imitated by native artists."[2]

Julius Caesar, when he invaded Britain about the middle of the first century B.C., found gold coins circulating in the island. Concerning the Britons he said:[3] "They use either bronze or gold coins or instead of coined money tallie of iron, of a certain weight." Gold coins, it is known, were struck by Cunobelin (Shakespeare's Cymbeline), a king of Britons, in the first half of the first century A.D.[4]

Even for those early days in Britain there is evidence of debasements of gold coins. These British coins varied in weight from about 120 grains to 84 grains, gradually becoming lighter as time went on.[5]

After Caesar's conquest of Britain, the influence of Roman art on these British coins became pronounced and British money was in large part super-

[1] HAWKINS, EDWARD, *The Silver Coins of England*, p. 9.
[2] *Ibid.*, pp. 9–10.
[3] CAESAR, GAIUS JULIUS, *Commentarii de bello Gallico*, Bk. V, Chap. 12.
[4] HAWKINS, EDWARD, *op. cit.*, pp. 14–15.
[5] KENYON, *op. cit.*, p. 1.

seded by Roman coins. A Roman edict ultimately demanded "that all money current in this island should bear the image and superscription of the Roman Emperor."[1] The Romans maintained their control of Britain until the fifth century and then abandoned the country entirely.

Very little is known about the coins of England from early in the fifth century until the eighth century. Kenyon believes that during that period some coins were struck there both of gold and of silver.[2]

According to *Beowulf*, the Anglo-Saxons of the ninth century used rings of gold and of silver to some extent as media of exchange and rough measures of value.

At the accession of William I (1066), silver was the principal money of England and continued to be so until early in the eighteenth century. The monetary pound at first weighed a pound of standard silver. According to Lord Liverpool,[3]

. . . the Pound in tale of the Silver Coins . . . was equal to the Pound weight of standard Silver, that is, the Tower Pound [of 5400 grains]. . . . The Pound in tale, which was then also a pound in weight, was divided into twenty Shillings, and each Shilling into twelve Pence or Sterlings.[4] The Pound weight was

---

[1] HAWKINS, *op. cit.*, p. 16.

[2] KENYON, *op. cit.*, p. 3.

[3] LIVERPOOL, CHARLES JENKINSON, 1st Earl of, *A Treatise on the Coins of the Realm in a Letter to the King*, p. 35.

[4] The origin of the word *sterling* is uncertain. It probably has reference to a Norman penny having a star (*steorra*) on one side.

divided into twelve ounces, and each ounce into twenty penny-weights; so that each Penny or Sterling weighed one penny-weight or twenty-four grains.

After the end of the ninth century, no gold coinage took place either in England or in any of the neighboring countries until the time of Henry III. The gold bezants of the Greek Empire and the gold coins struck during the ninth and tenth centuries by the Arabic princes in Sicily were probably used more or less in mercantile transactions all over Europe, but they were not legal currency in England and were probably passed merely as bullion.

From the Reign of Henry III to the Discovery of America

Upon approaching modern times, we find that the first gold coin struck in England was the penny of pure gold made by Henry III in 1257.[1] It weighed 45 grains, or $\frac{1}{120}$ of a Tower pound. With its in-

---

[1] The reintroduction of gold money into the circulation of Europe after its nearly complete absence for about eight centuries is a fact of importance in the world's subsequent economic history. It can be traced largely to the influence of the Crusades, and the contacts they effected between the West and the gold-bearing and gold-money-using East—notably Byzantium. The resulting growth of trade between the West and the East and its need for a more convenient medium of payment than silver were conducive to the reintroduction of gold money in the West. This new western coinage of gold appeared almost simultaneously in the commercial cities of Italy and in France and Germany. The first of these gold coins was apparently the florin, issued by the Republic of Florence in 1252. In the same year gold coins were issued in Genoa. The French series of gold coins was begun in 1254 by Louis IX, probably having been a result of the Sixth Crusade, which he had led 5 years before. About the same time, Emperor Frederick II minted a gold coin at Naples.

troduction, the practices were inaugurated of giving gold coins a fixed rating with the silver coins then in general circulation and of making them legally current at the official rating.[1] This new gold penny was rated to pass as equivalent to 20 "sterlings," or silver pennies, giving a gold-silver ratio of 10 to 1. It was called a *penny* because this word was then the common term for money in general. The French, or Norman, equivalent of penny was *denier,* and to this day the English abbreviation for penny is *d.*

The idea of the gold coinage in England in 1257, under Henry III, appears to have been derived from that of St. Louis of France.[2] Neither in England nor in France, however, was the first gold coinage a success.[3]

In England the period was not a propitious one for a coin of a denomination so high as that of the gold penny. Times were hard and food prices were high. The Mad Parliament was about to meet. Late in the year 1257, after the coins had been in circulation only a few months, the city of London sent to the King a protest against these coins, to which the King responded by a proclamation declaring that no one was required to accept the coins and that anyone who should accept them was authorized to bring them to his exchange, where they would be redeemed

---

[1] LIVERPOOL, *op. cit.,* p. 45.

[2] SHAW, W. A., *The History of Currency,* 1252–1894, p. 11.

[3] KENYON, *op. cit.,* pp. 14–15.

in silver coins at their current value, with only a small charge[1] for their redemption. Apparently not many of these gold pennies were struck. Nonetheless, they continued to be current and the records show that in 1265 their rating in terms of silver coins was raised from 20 pence to 24 pence.

After this premature gold coinage of Henry III, there is no evidence of any further coining of gold in England until 1343.[2] The period of nearly a century, however, was one of great commercial expansion in Europe. Gold coins were being used in northern Italy, in France, and in Flanders, the countries with which England was conducting her principal commerce.[3] It was, moreover, a period of scarcity of the precious metals, accompanied by declining commodity prices—an evil not remedied until the arrival of the new supplies of gold and silver acquired through the discovery of America.

In 1343, therefore, in order to facilitate foreign trade and to check falling prices by increasing the supply of money in the kingdom, the Council, after an examination before Parliament of a number of goldsmiths, moneyers and merchants, resolved that a single kind of gold money should be made both in England and in Flanders, if the Flemings were willing, and that the money should be current in both countries (to the exclusion of all other gold coins), on

[1] *Ibid.*

[2] RUDING, ROGERS, *Annals of the Coinage of Great Britain and Its Dependencies*, vol. I, p. 216.

[3] KENYON, *op. cit.*, pp. 16–17.

such conditions as should be determined by the King in Council. Following this resolution, an indenture was made authorizing three gold coins, the florin, the half florin, and the quarter florin. A florin was to be of the weight of two *petit florins* of Florence (108 grains) and of the same fineness (23 carats 3½ grains pure gold to ½ grain alloy) and was to be rated at 6 shillings. It was equivalent to 1½ solidi or aurei. This gold florin was made current in 1343.

This second attempt within a century, however, to produce a gold coinage for England failed. It was soon found that the gold coins at the official rating of 12.61 to 1, a rating copied from the one then prevailing in France, were undervalued in terms of silver coins and therefore did not continue in circulation. Accordingly, a proclamation was issued in July, 1344, providing that these gold coins should be taken thereafter only with the consent of the person to whom they were offered. The following month, another proclamation declared that they were to be accepted only according to their value as gold bullion.[1]

The date of the first official entry that has been preserved of gold's being brought by the public to the mint for coinage is in 1345.[2]

With the facilitating of trade with Flanders and the remedying of the difficulties experienced with the

[1] KENYON, *op. cit.*, pp. 16–17.
[2] RUDING, *op. cit.*, vol. I, p. 61.

underrated florin as its principal objects, the Government in 1344 introduced a new gold coin called a *noble*, which contained 138⅝₁₃ grains of gold, *i.e.*, 28.2 per cent more gold than the florin, and was rated at 6 shillings 8 pence, as contrasted with the florin's 6 shillings.[1] The regular coinage of gold now began.

In 1346 the noble was debased by about 7 per cent, to 128⅘₇ grains; in 1353 it was again debased, this time also by about 7 per cent, to 120 grains; then, in 1414 it was debased by 10 per cent, to 108 grains. In 1460 its gold content was raised by about 11 per cent, from 108 grains to 120 grains, but its declared value was raised by about 43 per cent, *i.e.*, from 6 shillings 8 pence to 8 shillings 4 pence,[2] representing a further debasement of about 32 per cent.

Ten years later the noble was replaced by a coin called, from the emblem it bore, the *angel*. This coin was given the same declared gold value of 6 shillings 8 pence that the noble of the earlier mintages had had—a reduction of 30 per cent—but it was reduced in weight to 80 grains of gold, or by 33⅓ per cent, representing a debasement of 3⅓ per cent from the preceding coinage of 1460.

These repeated debasements were in large part attempts to solve two currency problems: (1) the differences continually arising between official gold and silver ratings and the market-value ratios of the two metals and (2) the fact that both gold and

[1] Shaw, *op. cit.*, p. 44; also, Kenyon, *op. cit.*, pp. 18–19.
[2] Shaw, *op. cit.*, p. 44.

silver coins were for a large part of the time in a bad condition as a result of abrasion, sweating, clipping, boring, scraping, and counterfeiting. Furthermore, since the ratings of gold and silver coins were frequently different in some of the Continental countries from what they were in England, there was a continual draining of the better preserved coins and of the undervalued metal out of one country and into another—the coin and the metal always tending to move from the places where they were cheap to the places where they were dear; in other words, always seeking the best market. In pursuance of this principle, the bad money was always driving out the good money.

Summarizing an excellent account of the period 1300 to 1492, in Europe, Shaw says:[1]

The characteristics of this period are perfectly well defined, and repeat themselves with almost faithful and exact similarity of recurrence in the several states comprising the Europe of that date. In brief, such characteristics were those of (1) a period of commercial expanse, necessitating an increasing currency and advancing prices; (2) a period of stationary production of the precious metals, necessitating a struggle among the various states for the possession of those metals; (3) a period of endless change in the ratio between gold and silver, necessitating continual revision of the rate of exchange.

DEVELOPMENTS FROM 1492 TO 1821

The story of gold money in England from the discovery of America until near the end of the seven-

[1] SHAW, *op. cit.*, p. 13.

teenth century can be told briefly. This was a time of quasi bimetallism, in which both gold and silver coins were continually minted and enjoyed the same legal rights as money.

Silver Predominant over Gold for Two Centuries of Quasi Bimetallism

Generally throughout these two centuries the ratios were favorable to silver. Silver money, therefore, dominated. The condition of the coins, however, both silver and gold, was usually bad.[1] Accordingly, Gresham's law[2] worked in two ways: (1) The overvaluing of silver by the mint ratios resulted in a great predominance of silver coins in the circulation; and (2) the bad state of most of the silver and gold coins resulted in the exportation, melting, and hoarding of the better coins of both metals and in the retention in active circulation of the coins that were most defective by reason of having been clipped, sweated, filed, washed, and bored. The Government in its efforts to remedy this situation resorted frequently to recoinages involving a pro-

---

[1] *Cf.* pp. 38 and 46.

[2] Gresham's law is a term applied by H. D. McLeod in 1858 to the principle that when two kinds of money are in circulation side by side and one is inferior to the other, the inferior one under certain conditions will drive the superior one out of circulation. The discovery of the law is often attributed to Sir Thomas Gresham, who was an adviser to Queen Elizabeth on the reform of the currency. However, the principle was known, as we have seen, long before Gresham's time, and there is no evidence that he contributed anything new to the formulation of the law. For a fuller statement of the law, see pp. 135–136, note.

gressive debasement of both gold and silver money. The deterioration of the monetary standard was especially pronounced during the latter part of the reign of Henry VIII, throughout the reign of Edward VI, and again later, from about 1660 until near the end of the century. Sir Dudley North in his *Discourses upon Trade*, published in 1691, said:[1]

I call to witness the vast Sums that have been coyned in *England*, since the free Coynage was set up; What is become of it all? no body believes it to be in the Nation, and it cannot well be all transported, the Penalties for so doing being so great. The case is plain, it being exported, as I verily believe little of it is, the Melting-Pot devours all. . . .

And I know no intelligent Man who doubts, but the New Money goes this way.

Silver and Gold, like other Commodities, have their ebbings and flowings: Upon the arrival of Quantities from *Spain*, the Mint commonly gives the best price; that is, coyned Silver, for uncoyned Silver, weight for weight. Wherefore is it carried into the *Tower*, and coyned? not long after there will come a demand for Bullion, to be Exported again: If there is none, but all happens to be in Coyn, What then? Melt it down again; there's no loss in it, for the Coyning cost the Owners nothing.

Thus the Nation hath been abused, and made to pay for the twisting of straw, for Asses to eat.

Much of the currency that remained in circulation consisted of iron, brass, or copper pieces plated, and such coins as were of good silver were worth scarcely one-half their current value.[2]

[1] NORTH, SIR DUDLEY, *Discourses upon Trade*, pp. 29-30.
[2] SHAW, *op. cit.*, p. 223.

Such was the situation that led to the famous recoinage of 1696 to 1699,[1] to the plans for which the philosopher John Locke contributed much.

Gold Predominant over Silver for a Century

In the recoinage of 1696 to 1699 the gold-silver ratio was raised from about 15 to 1 to approximately 15½ to 1, making it unduly favorable to gold and thereby stimulating a heavy importation of foreign gold coins into England and their minting into British money; likewise, stimulating a heavy exportation and melting down of the undervalued British silver coins.[2]

This recoinage changed England's bimetallism to a monetary system dominated by gold from one dominated by silver, and such it continued to be until the suspension of specie payments near the end of the eighteenth century.

From 1702 to 1717, according to the reports of Sir Isaac Newton, Master of the Mint, the gold coined at the mint represented a value approximately thirty-two times that of the silver coined. To meet this situation and the resulting inconvenience to the public caused by a lack of small silver coins, Newton recommended a reduction in the gold-silver ratio from 15½ to 1 to approximately 15.21 to 1, and the recommendation was adopted. Although this brought a real improvement in the

[1] Cf. RUDING, op. cit., vol. II, pp. 40–51.
[2] SHAW, op. cit., pp. 226–227.

currency and an increase in the supply of silver money, monetary troubles continued.

The process of culling and exporting the heavier silver coins persisted, and by 1760 the silver coinage was in so imperfect a state that the crown pieces had almost entirely disappeared, although they had been minted since 1695 to the amount of over £1½ million sterling. Of the half crowns, minted to the value of £2⅓ million sterling, only defaced and impaired specimens remained current, while shillings and sixpences had lost every sign of impression. In discussing this experience, Shaw says:[1]

The idea that bimetallic action replaces one good metal by another, an equal weight of one metal for that of the other, a good undepreciated coinage of silver for a good undepreciated coinage of gold, or *vice versa*, is not borne out by a single instance in history. Bimetallic action always substitutes the less for the greater, whether weight or value, the more depreciated for the less, or the depreciated for the perfect standard coin.

The mint ratio, therefore, during the first three-quarters of the eighteenth century was favorable to gold and unfavorable to silver, thereby attracting the yellow metal into the circulation of England and repelling the white metal. At the same time, however, the gold coins were rendered so defective by continual clipping, boring, sweating, and filing that such gold coins as continued to be in good condition were melted and exported.[2]

[1] SHAW, *op. cit.*, pp. 231–233.
[2] *Ibid.*, pp. 234–235.

To solve this problem, the House of Commons on May 10, 1774, passed a resolution that declared:

. . . considerable quantities of old silver coin of this realm, or coin purporting to be such, greatly below the standard of the Mint in weight, have been lately imported into this kingdom, and it is expedient that some provision should be made to prevent the practice.

The lower house, therefore, prohibited the importation of light silver coin into the kingdom and ordered the confiscation of it in case of discovery, while further providing

that no tender in the payment of money made in the silver coin of the realm, of any sum exceeding the sum of £25 at any one time, shall be reputed in law or allowed to be a legal tender within Great Britain or Ireland for more than according to its value by weight, after the rate of 5s. 2d. per oz of silver, and no person to whom such tender shall be made shall be any way bound thereby or obliged to receive the same in payment in any manner than as aforesaid; any law, statute, or usage to the contrary notwithstanding.

This limitation on the legal-tender quality of silver money by tale was the beginning of the end of bimetallism in England.

The Paper Pound

Between 1793 and 1797 gold coins of the denominations of one guinea (21 shillings), a half guinea, and a third of a guinea were in general circulation. There were no coins representing a pound sterling, but the equivalent of a pound was recognized as 123¼ grains of gold ¹¹⁄₁₂ fine. The coinage of gold at the mint was free and gratuitous. Although the exportation of English gold coins and of gold obtained from the melting down of these coins was forbidden by law, the law was extensively flouted. At times when gold was moving out of England, there developed a premium on legally exportable bullion and foreign gold coin. This premium was small. Referring to it, Bosanquet, in his *Practical Observations Concerning the Report of the Bullion Committee*, said in 1810, "The conscience of the exporter and the value of a false oath [regarding the origin of the gold being exported] are correctly stated by the Committee at 4½ per cent."

Bank Notes and Deposit Currency

The paper money of England in 1797 consisted of bank notes—those of the Bank of England, which circulated for the most part in London and the vicinity, and those of the "country" banks, which circulated chiefly in their respective communities. Notes were redeemable in specie on demand, but were not legal tender.

There were no restrictions on the receipt of deposits by banks in England and their circulation by means of bank checks; and during the latter half of the eighteenth century and the early nineteenth century the use of deposit currency was increasing.[1]

---

[1] *Bullion Committee Report*, p. 151; also, Sir John Lubbock, On the Country Clearings, *Journal of the Statistical Society*, vol. XXVIII (1865), pp. 361*ff.*

England was on a *de facto* paper-money standard from 1797 to 1821, although in 1816 she enacted the legislation that 5 years later placed her squarely on the gold standard. England's 24 years' experience with a paper-money standard are important to the student of money for two reasons: (1) They represent an experiment with a managed paper-money standard by an advanced nation, and (2) they gave rise to the so-called *bullion controversy*, in which David Ricardo was an active participant, and to the Bullion Report, which gave the world a classic presentation of certain monetary theories, which at the time were understood by very few persons, but which later became the world's "orthodox" philosophy of money.[1]

Our present study of the gold standard is not concerned with this paper-money-standard period, except to the extent of noting briefly how the preceding metallic-money standard broke down and how the new gold standard was born.

In February, 1793, England declared war on France. After beginnings favorable to England and her allies early in 1793, the tide of war turned, and during the next few years the French were almost continually victorious. By 1797, England's allies had made separate treaties of peace with France, and England faced Napoleon alone. The military situation looked black. The internal economic situation during these 4 years was also unfavorable.

---

[1] On this subject see CANNAN, EDWIN, *The Paper Pound;* also, KEMMERER, EDWIN WALTER, *Money*, Chap. II.

Other factors that contributed directly to the suspension of specie payments were (1) the heavy demands made by the Government upon the Bank of England for advances with which to meet war expenditures—many of which required the transfer of large sums to the continent; (2) the pull on British gold and silver resulting from a return of France to a specie basis after her disastrous paper-money inflation with the assignats and mandats. During the early years of this inflation, specie had flowed in large quantities to England from France and other neighboring countries for safety. With the conclusion of the French Revolution, the restoration of law and order, and the return of France to a bimetallic currency, much of this specie was drawn home again; (3) the uncertain political situation in Britain, which contributed to heavy demands on the Bank of England for specie.

By the spring of 1795, exchange in London on the principal Continental cities reached the gold-export point and a strong outward movement of specie to Paris, Hamburg, and Lisbon took place. This gold drain so reduced the reserves of the Bank of England that the directors notified Pitt in February, 1797, that the situation was desperate. The Prime Minister responded on February 26 with a council resolution providing that

the Directors of the Bank of England should forbear issuing any cash in payment until the sense of Parliament can be taken on that subject and the proper measures adopted thereupon for maintaining the means of circulation and supporting the public and commercial credit of the Kingdom . . .

Under this resolution the redemption of Bank of England notes in specie was suspended and the nation went over to a depreciated paper-money standard, which continued until 1821. Some gold and silver coins, most of which were apparently very defective, continued in circulation, usually at premiums in terms of bank notes, although both the Bank of England and the Government made repeated efforts to prevent such premiums.[1]

Throughout most of the period of the suspension there were heavy exports of both gold and silver coins,[2] and the scarcity of silver coins in particular caused great inconvenience to the public.

Lord Liverpool's Letter to the King

At the time of suspension in 1797, as we have seen, the coins of the realm were in a bad state, particularly the silver coins, of which the good ones had been exported and melted down in large quantities, and of which the poor ones remaining in circulation were badly clipped, sweated, and worn. To meet this situation, a committee of the Privy Council was appointed in 1798 to inquire into the state of the coins and to make recommendations for its improvement.

The most important member of this committee was

[1] See RUDING, *op. cit.*, vol. II, pp. 96, 107, 108, and 110.
[2] See SHAW, *op. cit.*, p. 241.

the first Earl of Liverpool, who, in cooperation with George Chalmers, drafted a report for the Privy Council in that year. This Letter to the King was not published until 1805,[1] by reason of the fact that Liverpool had been ill for several years. He died in 1808. The letter contained valuable historical and descriptive material concerning British money, a very able discussion of the principles of money, and a program for monetary reform.[2]

Here are strong and well-reasoned recommendations for the discontinuance of bimetallism and for the definitive adoption of a single gold standard. Lord Liverpool said:

Coins should be made of metals more or less valuable [*e.g.*, copper, silver, and gold], in proportion to the wealth and commerce of the country in which they are to be the measure of property.

In very rich countries, and especially in those where great and extensive commerce is carried on, Gold is the most proper metal. . . . In such countries Gold will in practice become the principal measure of property, and the instrument of commerce, with the general consent of the people, not only without the support of law, but in spite of almost any law that may be enacted to the contrary; for the principal purchases and exchanges cannot there be made, with any convenience, in Coins of a less valuable metal.[3]

[1] LIVERPOOL, *op. cit.*

[2] J. R. McCulloch said of this letter, "A more comprehensive and elaborate exposition of the principles on which the coinage should be conducted than is perhaps to be found in any other publication." (In PALGRAVE, *Dictionary of Political Economy*, vol. II, p. 616.)

[3] LIVERPOOL, *op. cit.*, p. 162.

Briefly summarized, Liverpool's recommendations for England were[1]

First, That the Coins of this realm, which are to be the principal measure of property and instrument of commerce, should be made of one metal only.

Secondly, That in this kingdom the Gold Coins only have been for many years past, and are now, in the practice and opinion of the people, the principal measure of property and instrument of commerce.

. . . Silver and Copper Coins should continue to be subservient to, and representative of, these Gold Coins, as they are at present. . . .

According to the plan I have proposed, the new Silver Coins will not be legal tender for any sum exceeding the nominal value of the largest piece of Gold Coin in currency.

Liverpool recommended that silver coins should contain less than their full value of silver bullion, *i.e.*, should be token coins. If it should be found necessary, in order to prevent counterfeiting, he submitted the question as to

whether it may not be advisable, that the Legislature should vest in Your Majesty, or such others as may be authorized by Your royal licence, (these will probably always be the Directors of the Bank of England,) the sole right of carrying Silver to your Mint to be coined: Your Majesty will thus have it in your power to limit and regulate the quantity of Silver Coins, which may at any time be sent into circulation . . .

Gold Standard Legally Adopted

In 1816 the old Currency Committee of the Privy Council, of which Lord Liverpool had been a member,

[1] *Ibid.*, pp. 170, 178, and 187.

was still in existence, although during the war the committee had refrained from making any recommendations. The war having ended with the battle of Waterloo in June, 1815, the committee was asked for a report, which it made in May, 1816, and in which it adopted Lord Liverpool's original proposals. It recommended a monometallic gold standard, continuing the existing weights and denominations of gold coins, with the coinage of gold free and gratuitous. Silver coins, it recommended, should thereafter be made subsidiary, slightly underweight, and with their legal-tender quality limited to 2 guineas.

Parliament promptly adopted the committee's recommendations in the Gold Standard Act of 1816 (Act 56, George III, chap. 68). The preamble of this act declared:

Whereas the silver coins of the realm have, by long use and other circumstances, become greatly diminished in number and deteriorated in value, so as not to be sufficient for the payments required in dealings under the value of the current gold coins, by reason whereof a great quantity of light and counterfeit silver coin and foreign coin has been introduced into circulation within this realm, and the evils resulting therefrom can only be remedied by a new coinage of silver money . . . And whereas at various times heretofore the coins of this realm of gold and silver have been usually a legal tender for payments to any amount, and great inconvenience has arisen from both these precious metals being concurrently the standard measure of value and equivalent of property, it is expedient that the gold coin made according to the indentures of the Mint should henceforth be the sole standard measure of value and legal tender for payment, without any limitation of amount, and that the silver coin should be a legal tender to a limited amount only, for the facility of exchange and commerce.

Provision was made for the withdrawal from circulation and the prompt recoinage of the old silver coins.

During the period of the suspension, the bank note depreciated to a maximum discount of approximately 27 per cent in terms of gold in 1813, and then, after 1815, rapidly rose toward par. Commodity prices in England had risen about 40 per cent by 1814 and then had declined.[1]

By the fall of 1816, the premium on gold for a short time reached a figure below 1 per cent, and the bank directors, in preparation for resumption of gold payments, slowly began to take positive action for increasing their stock of gold. In December they decided to experiment, in order to find out how much gold the public would demand if specie payments were resumed. Under authority of a provision in a law of 1797, they began to feel their way by offering to redeem, on demand, notes of small denomination that had been issued before certain specified dates. Few notes were presented for redemption. Encouraged by this fact, in the fall of 1817 they offered to redeem, on demand, in gold, notes of all denominations bearing dates of

[1] SILBERLING, NORMAN J., British Prices and British Cycles, 1779–1850, *The Review of Economic Statistics*, Supplement, 1923.

issue prior to January 1, 1817. This offer led to heavy demands for redemption and was soon withdrawn.

Although gold coins of 20 shillings had been coined as early as 1489 and "sovereigns" had been minted from time to time in the past, dating back as early as 1485, during this long period the sovereign had been of comparatively little importance. For about a century and a half the guinea had been England's most important gold coin.[1] An act of 1817 now replaced the guinea and its gold fractions by a new sovereign (and a half sovereign) representing 20 shillings to the sovereign and containing 123.27 grains of standard gold ($1\frac{1}{12}$ fine), *i.e.*, 113.00 grains of fine gold.

The Gold Standard Goes into Operation

Early in 1819 both houses of Parliament appointed secret committees to consider the question of resumption. The two committees finally agreed in recommending that the bank, after February 1, 1820, should be required to redeem notes in gold bullion on a specified scale of declining prices for gold, which would culminate in full cash payment not later than May 1, 1823. This provision for returning to full redemption over a period of time

---

[1] For the interesting story of the changing ratings of the "guinea" in terms of silver, following down the progressive debasements of the silver coins from 1670 through the coinage reform of John Locke in 1698 and that of Sir Isaac Newton in 1717, when the guinea was rated at 21 shillings, where it remained until 1816, see Guinea in Palgrave's *Dictionary of Political Economy*.

through a system of graduated rates never came into effect. Before February, 1820, the gold premium had entirely disappeared and on May 1, 1821, cash payments at parity were fully resumed.

Thus, after a paper-money regime of approximately a quarter of a century, England found herself back upon a metallic-money standard—but now upon a gold standard and not upon the legal bimetallic standard she had left in 1797.

On the basis of the legislation of 1816 and 1817, England's gold standard functioned after the return to specie payments in 1821 until the outbreak of the First World War, in 1914. Throughout this long period of 93 years, specie payments in gold were maintained, there was free coinage of gold, and the yellow metal moved out of England and into England without legal restrictions, going out when exchange reached the gold-export point and coming in when it reached the gold-import point. The system was highly automatic. There were no important changes in Britain's monetary standard for these three generations, except those incident to changes in the value or purchasing power of gold itself—a subject that will be discussed later.[1] There were many significant developments in the nation's banking and credit systems, notably those centering in the Peal Act of 1844, but these developments do not fall within the scope of this book.

The gold standard in England from 1821 to 1914,

---

[1] See pp. 188–194.

therefore, calls for very little historical discussion. Generally speaking, it functioned in an orthodox way, accompanied by many important developments in the bank-note and deposit-currency structure, which do not concern us here. Its significant features will be considered in Chaps. V to VII, in connection with the discussions of the theory and functioning of the gold standard. Concerning this gold-standard history, one can quote without much qualification Carlyle's well-known aphorism, "Happy the people whose annals are blanks in history books."

SELECTED BIBLIOGRAPHY

ANDRÉADÈS, A.: *History of the Bank of England*, P. S. King & Son, Ltd., London, 1909.

BULLION COMMITTEE: *Report from the Select Committee on the High Price of Bullion. Ordered by the House of Commons to be Printed 8th June*, 1810, London. [See also Cannan, Edwin, Editor.]

CAESAR, GAIUS JULIUS: *The Gallic War*, trans. by H. J. Edwards, Loeb Classical Library, G. P. Putnam's Sons (Knickerbocker Press), New York, 1919.

CANNAN, EDWIN, Editor: *The Paper Pound of 1797–1821*, a reprint of the Bullion Committee Report, P. S. King & Son, Ltd., London, 1919.

CARLILE, WILLIAM WARRAND: *The Evolution of Modern Money*, Macmillan & Company Ltd., London, 1901.

DEL MAR, A.: *A History of the Precious Metals*, George Bell & Sons, Ltd., London, 1880.

FEAVEARYEAR, A. E.: *The Pound Sterling—A History of English Money* (with Bibliography), Clarendon Press, Oxford University Press, New York, 1931.

GRUEBER, H. A.: *Handbook of the Coins of Great Britain and Ireland in the British Museum*, British Museum, London, 1899.

HAWKINS, EDWARD: *The Silver Coins of England*, Edward Lumley, London, 1841.

HAWTREY, R. G.: *Currency and Credit*, Longmans, Green and Company, New York, 1930.

————: *The Gold Standard in Theory and Practice*, Longmans, Green and Company, New York, 1927.

International Monetary Conference of 1878: *Report*, Government Printing Office, Washington, D.C., 1879.

JACOB, WILLIAM: *An Historical Inquiry into the Production and Consumption of the Precious Metals*, 2 vols., John Murray, London, 1831.

JEVONS, W. STANLEY: *Investigations in Currency and Finance*, Macmillan & Company, Ltd., London, 1909.

KEMMERER, EDWIN WALTER: *Money*, The Macmillan Company, New York, 1935.

KENYON, ROBERT LLOYD: *The Gold Coins of England*, Bernard Quaritch, London, 1884.

LEAKE, STEPHEN MARTIN: *An Historical Account of English Money*, 2d ed., W. Meadows, London, 1745.

LIVERPOOL, CHARLES JENKINSON, 1st Earl of: *A Treatise on the Coins of the Realm; in a Letter to the King*, E. Wilson, London, 1880.

McCULLOCH, J. R., Editor: *Old and Scarce Tracts on Money*, P. S. King & Son, Ltd., London, 1933.

MARTIN, JOHN BIDDULPH: Seigniorage and Mint Charges, *Journal of the Institute of Bankers*, V, 1884.

NEWTON, SIR ISAAC: *Representations on the Subject of Money*, 1711–1712 and 1717, published in J. R. McCulloch's *Old and Scarce Tracts on Money*, P. S. King & Son, Ltd., London, 1933.

NICHOLSON, J. SHIELD: *A Treatise on Money and Monetary Problems*, 3d ed., A. & C. Black, Inc., London, 1895.

NORTH, SIR DUDLEY: *Discourses upon Trade*, 1691. Reprinted and edited by Jacob H. Hollander, Lord Baltimore Press, Baltimore, Md., 1907.

PALGRAVE, R. H. INGLIS, Editor: *Dictionary of Political Economy*, 3 vols., Macmillan & Company, Ltd., London, 1926.

————: The Gold Coinage, *Journal of the Institute of Bankers*, V, 1884.

RUDING, ROGERS: *Annals of the Coinage of Great Britain and Its Dependencies from the Earliest Period of Authentic History to the Reign of Victoria*, 3d ed., 3 vols., John Hearne, London, 1840.

SHAW, W. A.: *The History of Currency 1252–1894*, 2d ed., G. P. Putnam's Sons (Knickerbocker Press), New York, 1896.

SILBERLING, NORMAN J.: British Prices and Business Cycles 1779–1850, *The Review of Economic Statistics*, Prel. vol. V (1923), Supplement 2.

SNELLING, THOMAS: *A View of the Gold Coin of England from Henry the Third to the Present Time*, T. Snelling, London, 1763.

WALKER, FRANCIS A.: *International Bimetallism*, Henry Holt and Company, Inc., New York, 1897.

YOUNG, JOHN PARKE: *European Currency and Finance*, 2 vols., Government Printing Office, Washington, D.C., 1925.

CHAPTER III

Gold Money and the Gold Standard in the United States Prior to the First World War

American life storms about us daily and is slow to find a tongue.—RALPH WALDO EMERSON.

Gold monometallism did not actually exist in America until 1879. Nonetheless, from the beginning of European settlements here, gold, at least to some extent, has always served as basic money. Our experience with it may be divided into four periods: (1) the period prior to the National Mint Act of 1792, roughly, the preconstitutional period, during which only a scattering of gold money circulated in the country, along with many silver and copper coins and with large amounts of inconvertible paper money; (2) the period of bimetallism, from 1792 to the long suspension of specie payment at the end of 1861 (omitting the brief suspension from 1814 to 1817); (3) the period of the greenback standard, from 1862 through 1878, during which the only circulation of gold money of consequence was a limited amount on the Pacific Coast, although gold performed secondary monetary functions elsewhere; (4) the period of the gold standard, from the resumption of specie payments in 1879 to the First World War.

THE PRECONSTITUTIONAL PERIOD

The Colonial Period

Gold money circulated in North America to a small extent from early in the seventeenth century, along with many varieties of the more abundant Spanish milled dollars and their fractions, some other foreign coins, and a few locally minted silver and copper coins. Gold money, however, did not play an important role in America prior to the national period.

No gold was minted in America in this early period, and there was no gold-mining industry. Gold coins were brought into the colonies by migrants from the homelands; and some gold came in from England, France, Holland, Spanish countries, and especially the West Indies, as a result of trade with them. Inasmuch as these gold coins were of widely varying denominations and were often greatly underweight, by reason of having been clipped, scraped, or otherwise tampered with, they passed by weight and not by count.

The information that has come down to us concerning this early gold money is meager. A few items culled from various sources will suggest the broad outlines of the picture.

During the seventeenth century, the Portuguese

found placer gold in Brazil and carried large quantities of it to Portugal, whence it moved by trade routes to other parts of the world, including America.[1] According to Crosby,[2] the old English gold nobles and marks were sometimes made use of, at least by name, in the colonies between 1645 and 1690. Chalmers says[3] that prior to 1704 gold coins in the American colonies "were of rare occurrence and were regarded as counters rather than as real money." During the eighteenth century gold replaced silver as the dominant metallic standard in the English West Indies, which received much gold from Portuguese and Spanish sources and also some from the American colonies, by offering ratings giving preference to gold over silver.[4]

A British law of 1750 mentions a number of gold coins as circulating in Massachusetts Bay Colony, including British guineas, crowns, and half crowns, and the double and single Johannes and moidore of Portugal. In 1752 Massachusetts treasury bonds were made payable in silver or gold, at a fixed ratio of equivalence, and gold coins were current in the province. A large amount of gold was shipped in 1758 from England to Massachusetts in payment of subsidies voted by Parliament; and 4 years later the Massachusetts legislature declared that "gold

[1] DEL MAR, A., *A History of the Previous Metals*, p. 336; also Charles J. Bullock, *Monetary History of the United States*, pp. 13–14.

[2] CROSBY, S. S., *Early Coins of America*, p. 30.

[3] CHALMERS, ROBERT, *A History of Currency in the British Colonies*, p. 10.

[4] International Monetary Conference of 1878, *Report*, pp. 418–419.

is now become by far the greatest part of the medium of trade in this Province."[1]

The Period of the Revolution and the Confederation

In 1776 the Continental Congress appointed a committee to examine

. . . the value of the several species of Gold and Silver Coins, current in these Colonies, and the proportions they ought to bear to Spanish milled dollars.

Shortly afterward, following the recommendation of this committee, it was

Resolved, That the several Gold and Silver Coins passing in the said Colonies shall be received into the public treasury of the Continent, and paid out in exchange for bills emitted by the authority of Congress, when the same shall become due, at rates set down in the following table.[2]

It was further resolved that

. . . whoever shall offer, demand, or receive more in said bills for any Gold or Silver Coins or bullion, than at the rates aforesaid, or more of said bills for any lands houses goods wares or merchandise than the nominal sums at which the same might be purchased of the same person with Gold or Silver, every such person ought to be deemed an enemy to the liberties of these Colonies and treated accordingly . . .

[1] *Cf.* BULLOCK, *op. cit.*, p. 26; also, William G. Sumner, *A History of American Currency*, p. 41.

[2] The table gives rates for 12 different gold coins of British, French, Portuguese, and Spanish origin. International Monetary Conference, *op. cit.*, pp. 421–422.

Robert Morris, in his coinage scheme proposed in 1782, said:[1]

. . . where coins are so numerous [as they are now in America] that the knowledge of them is a kind of science, the lower order of citizens are constantly injured by those, who carry on the business of debasing, sweating, clipping, counterfeiting, and the like . . . Experience has already told us, that the advantage of Gold as a coin, is in this country very considerably diminished; for every distinct piece must be weighed before it can be safely received.

Coinage Plans Proposed. Between the end of the colonial period, July 4, 1776, and the beginning of the national government, April 30, 1789, several coinage plans for the new nation were proposed.

In 1782 Robert Morris, who was Superintendent of Finance in the Confederation from 1781 to 1784, recommended to the Congress a new coinage scheme. Morris believed that bimetallism would not work and that, for a single standard, silver was preferable to gold. He said:

Gold is more valuable than Silver, and so far must have the preference, but it is from that very circumstance the more exposed to fraudulent practices. Its value rendering it more portable is an advantage, but it is an advantage, which paper possesses in a much greater degree, and of consequence the commercial nation of England has had recourse to paper for the purposes of its Trade; although the mass of circulating Coins is Gold. It will always be in our power to carry a paper circulation to every proper extent. There can be no doubt,

[1] International Monetary Conference, 1878, pp. 426–427.

therefore, that our money standard ought to be affixed to Silver.

At the time that Robert Morris made his recommendation to Congress, Thomas Jefferson prepared a memorandum on the subject, which was likewise sent to Congress.[1] Jefferson favored basing the monetary unit on the value of the Spanish milled dollar, with which the public was thoroughly familiar, and adopting a bimetallic system. "It is not impossible," he said, "that 15 for 1 may be found an eligible proportion. I state it however as conjectural only."

The Continental Congress received, on May 13, 1785, the report of its Grand Committee on the Money Unit, which recommended a bimetallic system with a monetary unit equivalent in value to the existing Spanish milled dollar (estimated at 362 grains of fine silver), a gold-silver ratio of 15 to 1, and monetary denominations based on the decimal system. The Congress took the committee's report under consideration about 2 months later and, by unanimous vote, resolved merely that the monetary unit should be one dollar, that the smallest coin should be made of copper, of which 200 should pass for one dollar, and that the several pieces should increase in a decimal ratio.

In the following year, on April 8, the Board of the Treasury, consisting of Samuel Osgood and Walter Livingston, proposed to the Congress a coinage

[1] *Ibid.*, pp. 437–443.

system. Their reports, which were threefold, recommended the silver equivalent of the Spanish milled dollar as the monetary unit, the coinage of standard coins of both silver and gold, and the decimal system of denominations. Congress responded on August 8, 1786, to the board's recommendation by a resolution offering a detailed coinage plan.[1] It provided that the monetary unit should be a dollar consisting of 375.64 grains of fine silver, that there should be a decimal system of coins, running from one mill to ten dollars, that the coins below a dime should be made of copper, that those from a dime to a dollar should be made of silver, and that there should be two gold coins. With reference to the latter, the resolution provided that one coin should contain 246.268 grains of fine gold, equal to $10; that it should be stamped with the impression of the American eagle, and be called an *eagle*. The other should contain 123.134 grains of fine gold, should be equal to $5, should be stamped in like manner, and be called a *half eagle*. The gold-silver ratio here recommended was approximately 15.25 to 1.

Although an ordinance was passed by the Continental Congress on October 16, authorizing the establishment of a mint and the coinage of gold, silver, and copper coins, nothing was accomplished in this direction until after the new national government was established.

[1] *Ibid.*, pp. 450–541.

A National Currency Established

Metallic Money and the Constitution. With the ratification of the Constitution, the national government was given power "to coin money, regulate the value thereof, and of foreign coin and fix the standard of weights and measure." This power was made exclusive by the provision that "no state shall . . . coin money; emit bills of credit; make anything but gold and silver coin a tender in payment of debts." The records of the Constitutional Convention and of the debate over the adoption of the Constitution show that there was practically no controversy over the provisions of the Constitution relating to coinage. They were everywhere taken for granted.

Our constitutional fathers were familiar with the fact that over many centuries the kings and other potentates of Europe had followed the practice of debasing the coins of the realm so as to make seigniorage profits for themselves or their governments. Adam Smith, in his *Wealth of Nations*[1] published in 1776 and widely read in this country during the years immediately following, had said, giving many historical examples:

When national debts have once been accumulated to a certain degree, there is scarce, I believe, a single instance of their having been fairly and completely paid. The liberation of the public revenue, if it has ever been brought about at all, has

---

[1] SMITH, ADAM, *The Wealth of Nations*, Bk. V, Chap. III.

always been brought about by a bankruptcy; sometimes by an avowed one, but always by a real one, though frequently by a pretended payment.

The raising of the denomination of the coin has been the most usual expedient by which a real public bankruptcy has been disguised under the appearance of a pretended payment. . . .

The honour of a state is surely very poorly provided for, when in order to cover the disgrace of a real bankruptcy, it has recourse to a juggling trick of this kind, so easily seen through, and at the same time so extremely pernicious.

Almost all states, however, ancient as well as modern, when reduced to this necessity have, upon some occasions, played this very juggling trick . . .

By means of such expedients the coin of, I believe, all nations has been gradually reduced more and more below its original value, and the same nominal sum has been gradually brought to contain a smaller and smaller quantity of silver.

The men who gave us our Constitution were fearful of placing excessive monetary powers in the hands of the executive, and therefore wisely placed the authority to regulate the value of the nation's money in the hands of Congress.

Hamilton's Report on the Mint. The House of Representatives, on April 15, 1790, passed a resolution ordering the Secretary of the Treasury to prepare and report to the House a plan for the establishment of a national mint.

In response to this resolution, Alexander Hamilton submitted to the House, on April 28, 1791, his Report on the Mint—a report that showed a remarkable understanding of the principles of monetary science.

[61]

After a broad discussion of the question of a proper coinage policy for the new nation, Hamilton undertook to answer six questions concerning the coinage. Only the first two of them demand much attention in this study of gold money,[1] *viz.*, (1) "What ought to be the nature of the money unit of the United States?" and (2) "What the proportion between gold and silver, if coins of both metals are to be established?"

The Dollar Recommended as the Monetary Unit. Before answering the question of what the money unit ought to be, Hamilton undertook to answer the question, What is the money unit? He did so on the sound theory that the new unit ought, if practicable, to have a value very close to that of the existing one, so as to avoid disturbances in prices and wages and in the relations between debtors and creditors. He concluded that, although the pound was the unit in the money of account of all the states, the dollar was best entitled to be considered as the unit in the coins.

He then considered the fine-silver content of the principal Spanish dollars in circulation, concluding that the more ancient and more valuable dollars were not then to be found and "that the mass of

---

[1] The other four questions were (3) "What the proportion and composition of alloy in each kind?" (4) "Whether the expense of coinage shall be defrayed by the Government, or out of the material itself?" (5) "What shall be the number, denominations, sizes, and devices of the coins?" (6) "Whether foreign coins shall be permitted to be current or not; if the former, at what rate, and for what period?"

those generally current is composed of the newest and most inferior kinds." He decided that the present unit was somewhere between a dollar of about 368 grains of fine silver and one of about 374 grains.

Approaching the problem from another angle, he found the market ratio of gold to silver to be approximately 15 to 1. Multiplying the fine-gold equivalent of the dollar, *viz.*, 24¾ grains, by 15, he arrived at 371¼ grains of silver for the dollar—almost exactly the average of the fine-silver weights of Spanish dollars of the two more recent issues.

Hamilton in Favor of Bimetallism. The next question considered was whether the new coinage system should be silver monometallism, gold monometallism, or bimetallism. Up to that time, he said, the suggestions and proceedings had had for their object the annexing of the future money unit "emphatically to the silver dollar." Despite these prevailing ideas, however, he declared himself as "upon the whole, strongly inclined to the opinion, that a preference ought to be given to neither of the metals for the money unit," and that, "perhaps, if either were to be preferred, it ought to be gold rather than silver." "Gold," he said, "may, perhaps, in certain services, be said to have greater stability than silver; as, being of superior value, less liberties have been taken with it, in the regulations of different countries."

The value of gold, he thought, **was less likely** than that of silver to be influenced **by the circum-**

stances of commercial demand; and the revolutions that might take place in the comparative values of gold and silver in the future, he believed, would be more likely to be due to changes in the value of silver than in that of gold. However, these advantages of gold over silver he did not consider sufficient to justify the use of gold alone as a standard metal, and he concluded that "upon the whole, it seems to be most advisable . . . not to attach the unit exclusively to either of the metals; because this cannot be done effectually, without destroying the office and character of one of them as money, and reducing it to the situation of a mere merchandise . . . "

The use of the two metals as standard money, he thought, would also be of advantage in the development of the country's foreign trade, since "it is often, in the course of trade, as desirable to possess the kind of money, as the kind of commodities best adapted to a foreign market."

Hamilton then took up a study of what should be a proper mint ratio between gold and silver under his proposed bimetallic system. He recognized that the mint ratio should conform as nearly as possible to the market ratio in the leading markets of the world, and that, if a mint ratio materially different from the market ratio should be established, the over-valued metal would drive the undervalued metal out of circulation. After a lengthy discussion of the ratio question, he concluded, with some hesitation, that, all things considered, the best ratio to adopt would be 15 to 1.

On this basis Hamilton concluded "that the unit, in the coins of the United States, ought to correspond with 24 grains and ¾ of a grain of pure gold, and with 371 grains and ¼ of a grain of pure silver, each answering to a dollar in the money of account." Following the British practice, he favored making both gold and silver coins $^{11}\!/_{12}$ fine. He recommended the decimal system of notation. Six denominations of coins were recommended to begin with; *viz.*, gold pieces of ten dollars and of one dollar, silver pieces of one dollar and of ten cents, and copper pieces of one cent and of a half cent.

The question of whether a mint should impose a charge for the coining of gold and silver brought to it Hamilton discussed, reaching the conclusion that

under an impression that a *small* difference between the value of the coin and the mint price of bullion, is the least exceptionable expedient for restraining the melting down, or exportation of the former, and not perceiving that if it be a very moderate one, it can be hurtful in other respects—the Secretary is inclined to an experiment of one-half per cent on each of the metals.

As to foreign coins, Hamilton said the discontinuance of their circulation was a necessary part of the system contemplated for the new national coinage. He recommended, however, that the foreign coins should be "suffered to circulate, precisely upon their present footing, for one year after the mint shall

have commenced its operations," and that thereafter
their demonetization should be gradually extended
over a period of 2 years. It may be noted here,
parenthetically, that foreign coins were not actually
retired from circulation until about 65 years later.[1]

GOLD IN THE BIMETALLIC SYSTEM, 1792 TO 1861

The Mint Act of 1792. On April 2, 1792, after a
debate that was concerned chiefly with the questions
whether a representation of President Washington
should be stamped on the new gold coin, or an
emblem of liberty with the word *Liberty*, and whether
an eagle should be stamped on the reverse side of
the coin,[2] the Senate standing for the representation
of Washington and the House for the emblem of
liberty. The House won, and the mint bill became
law. In all important respects, save two, the Mint
Act followed the recommendations of Hamilton's
report. The two exceptions were (1) the adoption of a
slightly different fineness for the silver coins (*viz.*,
0.89240 instead of 0.91667)[3] and (2) the denominations of the coin to be minted. The act provided
for all the denominations recommended by Hamilton

[1] KEMMERER, EDWIN WALTER, *Money*, pp. 355–356; also Neil Carothers,
Fractional Money, p. 78.

[2] EVANS, GEORGE G., *History of the United States Mint and American Coinage*, p. 15.

[3] The object of this departure from Hamilton's recommendation was to
make the amount of alloy in the silver dollar such that, when added to the
371¼ grains of pure silver in the dollar, it would give the coin a gross weight
of 416 grains—the estimated approximate gross weight of the Spanish milled
dollars then in circulation.

except the gold dollar, but added gold pieces of five dollars and two dollars and a half, and silver pieces of fifty cents, twenty-five cents and five cents, thereby departing from the almost strictly decimal system of denominations recommended by Hamilton.

The copper cent and half-cent pieces authorized by the Mint Act and the subsequent act of May 8, 1792, carried practically their full value in their copper content, just as the gold and silver coins carried practically their full values in their weight of the respective metals.[1] Debasement of coins or embezzlement of metals by officers or employees of the mint was declared to be a felony and was punishable by death.

This law created in the United States a bimetallic system. Under it two kinds of standard money were linked together and both enjoyed exactly the same privileges under the law. Coins of both gold and silver were unlimited legal tender and were accepted in unlimited quantities by the government in payment of all taxes and other government dues. Both metals were coined at the mint on the same terms for persons taking them there for coinage, at the official ratio of 15 to 1.[2] This meant that, for a given weight of pure metal, fifteen times as many dollars of gold coins would be minted and paid back to the persons

[1] See CAROTHERS, op. cit., pp. 64–65.

[2] For the first 3 years, the director of the mint (contrary to law) put 374¾ grains of pure silver in a dollar of silver coin instead of 371¼ grains, as provided in the law, thereby making the effective ratio 15.14 to 1 instead of 15 to 1. The correct ratio was put into effect in November, 1795.

who brought gold as for the person who brought silver. In other words, for making money an ounce of gold was treated as worth fifteen times as much as an ounce of silver.

Gold Undervalued, 1792 to 1834

On July 31, 1792, the cornerstone was laid for a building in Philadelphia to be used as a mint—the first building to be erected by the new national government for public purposes. The work of coinage began in 1792 with the minting of a small amount of silver and copper coins. Gold coins were first struck in 1795.

The 15 to 1 ratio recommended by Hamilton and adopted in the Mint Act was at the time very close to the market ratio. This ratio, however, soon rose substantially above 15 to 1, and (with a few slight interruptions) remained at the higher level until 1833. From the year 1795, when the first United States gold coins were struck, to the end of 1833, the average of the 39 annual commercial ratios was 15.6 to 1.

This meant that, at the mint, gold was undervalued and silver was overvalued, as compared with the prices of the two metals prevailing in the bullion market, and also as compared with the coinage ratio of bimetallic France, which, from 1803 through 1833, was nominally 15½ to 1, but actually, when allowance was made for the coinage charges, was 15.69 to 1. The result of our low gold-silver ratio was that we got silver, which we overvalued, while gold, which we undervalued, went to France and elsewhere. The following chart gives a picture of what happened.

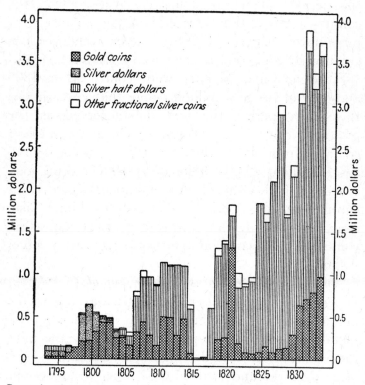

CHART 1.—Coinage of gold and silver at the United States Mint, 1793 to 1833. (Reproduced from Kemmerer, *Money*, page 337.)

At least some gold was coined in every year from 1795 to 1833 (except 1816 and 1817). During this period of 39 years, the United States minted approximately $15.5 million of gold coin, of which about two-thirds consisted of half eagles, slightly over 22 per cent consisted of eagles, and approximately 10 per cent consisted of quarter eagles. Throughout the period, silver predominated over gold in the country's circulation, and this predominance was pronounced between 1821 and 1833, when the circulation of gold coin in the country was very small.[1]

Since no silver dollars were coined after 1806 and only about $1.3 million before that year, during this entire period the half dollar served as the principal coin of the country. Of a total silver coinage from 1793 through 1833, amounting to $36.3 million, $33.0 million, or 90.9 per cent, consisted of half dollars.[2] All fractional silver coins throughout this period of American bimetallism were full weight, *i.e.*, a dollar in fractional coins contained the same amount of silver as a silver dollar.

American Silver Coins Forced Out of Circulation by Defective Foreign Silver Coins. Just as, during the greater part of this first period of American bimetallism, the silver coins, overvalued by the mint ratio of 15 to 1, were driving out of circulation on a large scale the undervalued gold coins, so, under the force of Gresham's law, were the badly worn, clipped,

---

[1] England's return to specie payment in 1821, with her adoption of gold monometallism, was an important cause of our large gold exportation beginning in that year.

[2] KEMMERER, *op. cit.*, pp. 337, 340, and 341; also, Carothers, *op. cit.*, pp. 75–76.

and otherwise defective foreign silver coins forcing out of circulation large amounts of the newly minted American silver coins.

The first of the coins to go was the silver dollar. Although it contained slightly less silver than an unworn Spanish milled dollar of more recent date, it contained more silver than the defective Spanish dollars usually found in circulation. The new American silver dollars were, therefore, quickly picked up and sent by trade channels to the West Indies, where they were popular by reason of their brightness and were readily exchanged for the heavier Spanish dollars that were in circulation there. These were then brought to the United States and put into circulation after some of the silver had been abstracted from them by clipping, scraping, boring, and sweating. The coinage of silver dollars was practically discontinued in 1805, not to be renewed until 1840.[1]

In the first third of the nineteenth century, therefore, both gold and silver coins were standard money, but silver strongly predominated under the newly established bimetallic standard. Our supply of coins was meager and their condition was unsatisfactory. There were few gold coins in active circulation and practically no American silver dollars. There were a substantial number of American half dollars, a few quarters and dimes, and an occasional half dime.

---

[1] Between 1806 and 1839, inclusive, the only silver dollars coined were, in 1805, $321; in 1836, $1,000; and in 1839, $300.

A large proportion of the coins in circulation consisted of clipped and badly worn foreign coins, especially coins of Spanish origin.

Agitation for Monometallism

By 1830, many thoughtful people were convinced that bimetallism would not work and that a system of monometallism should be adopted. A striking example of this attitude is found in the letters and reports of S. D. Ingham, who was Secretary of the Treasury during the first 2 years of Andrew Jackson's administration. In a report to the Senate under the date of May 4, 1830, Ingham said:[1]

> The proposition that there can be but one standard in fact is self-evident. The option of Governments charged with this duty is therefore between having property measured sometimes by gold and sometimes by silver, and selecting that metal which is best adapted to the purpose for the only standard. . . . The values of gold and silver, compared with each other, . . . are liable to fluctuations, resulting from the operations of human enterprise, the political convulsions of nations, and from the laws of nature, which can neither be anticipated, controlled nor averted. . . . A simple and certain remedy is within the reach of all. This remedy is to be found in the establishment of one standard measure of property only.

Although many at that time favored replacing bimetallism by a single standard, there was much difference of opinion as to whether that standard should be gold or silver. Secretary Ingham himself

[1] See International Monetary Conference, *op. cit.*, pp. 577 and 578.

favored the silver standard. He said[1] that "the standard measure of property should be made of a metal sufficiently abundant to enter into general circulation, determining values in small as well as large transactions." In a country like the United States, where most of the transactions of any size were performed by means of paper money, he thought that the absence of gold coins from circulation would not be a serious inconvenience. He pointed out that we had had long experience with a currency in which there was only a small amount of gold coin, but that we had had very little experience with a currency in which there was a dearth of silver coins. The inconvenience of the former, he said, had been slight but that of the latter would be serious. He thought that, if our silver coins should be drained off, their value would be supplied not by gold, but by small bank notes and tokens—"the worst species of paper currency."[2]

In opposition to the silver monometallists, advocates of the gold standard held that gold was preferable to silver as the standard money metal. They maintained that it was more stable in value and that, under a gold-standard system, silver could be kept in circulation in adequate quantities by the expedient of restricting the coinage of silver and of making silver coins token money with limited legal tender. They pointed to the success of the

[1] International Monetary Conference, *op. cit.*, p. 578.
[2] *Ibid.*, p. 577.

gold standard in England, with its token silver coinage, and to the desirability of our having a standard conforming to that of the country with which we carried on our largest trade.

The arguments of the gold monometallists were strengthened by the fact that, about that time, some gold discoveries were made in Georgia and North Carolina, which created in those sections special and local interests favorable to gold.

Bimetallism Continued

Nonetheless, the majority of thinking people still favored bimetallism, which appeared to them to be succeeding in France and which they believed had not been given a fair trial in the United States.

It had long been recognized that the mint ratio of 15 to 1 adopted by the United States in 1792 had soon thereafter fallen below the market ratio and also below the mint ratio of France. Agitation in favor of raising our mint ratio in order to restore our gold circulation became increasingly strong after 1828. A select committee of the House of Representatives, on the subject of the relative values of the gold and silver coins of the United States, made a report to the House on February 2, 1821, favoring an increase of our mint ratio to about 15.6 to 1. The committee found that[1] gold coins, both foreign and of the United States, had, in great

---

[1] *Finance Reports*, vol. III, pp. 660–661.

measure, disappeared; and, from the best calculation that could be made, there was reason to fear they would be wholly driven from circulation. There was no longer any doubt, they said, but that the gold coins of the United States were by our laws rated at a value lower than that in almost any other country, in comparison with that of silver.

Secretary of the Treasury Ingham made a long report to the Senate on May 4, 1830, on the question of the desirability of changing the ratio.[1] He said that, if bimetallism were to be continued and an effort made to restore gold to the circulation, probably the best ratio to adopt would be 15.625 to 1. The C. P. White Committee of the House, although preferring a single silver standard and desiring that gold coins, if they were placed in circulation at all, should be treated as subsidiary money, advocated in two reports the ratio of 15.625 to 1.

Despite all the reasons favorable to this ratio, which conformed closely to the French ratio, Congress hurriedly passed a law on June 28, 1834, adopting a ratio of 16.002 to 1. There was no explanation of this sudden change in its attitude. From a ratio unduly favorable to silver, Congress now suddenly jumped to the other extreme and adopted one unduly favorable to gold. The two reasons most commonly advanced were (1) that it was designed to help the gold-mining industry then developing in the southern slopes of the Allegheny

[1] See International Monetary Conference, *op. cit.*, pp. 558–662.

Mountains, and (2) that it would help drive out of circulation the notes of the Second Bank of the United States—an institution which at that time was meeting the vigorous opposition of President Jackson.

The legislation of this period left the pure-silver content of our silver coins unchanged. It effected the change in the gold-silver ratio by reducing the gross weight of a dollar of gold coin from 27 grains to 25.8 grains, and the pure-gold content from 24.75 grains to 23.2 grains. Each denomination of new gold coin, therefore, was given a gold content about 6.7 per cent less than under the old law. The new gold coins were given a millesimal fineness of 0.8992. This proved to be inconvenient to the mint and was accordingly raised by law to 0.900 in 1837. The change increased the pure-gold content of a dollar of gold coin from 23.2 grains to 23.22 grains—a gold content that was retained as long as gold coins were minted in the United States.

Since 1837, all our gold and silver coins (except the three-cent silver piece for a brief period)[1] have been 0.900 fine. The change in the gold coins made by the act of 1837 reduced the gold-silver value ratio at the mint from 16.002 to 1, established by the act of 1834, to 15.9884 to 1.

The act of 1834 made the old gold coins receivable in all payments at the rate of 94.8 cents per penny-weight, which was their bullion value in terms of the

[1] See pp. 81–82.

new gold coin, and at which value they were retired from circulation.

A reduction of 6.7 per cent in the amount of pure gold in a dollar of United States gold coin at most later periods in our history would have meant a substantial debasement of the currency. This was not the case, however, in 1834 to 1837, because at that time very few United States gold coins had been in circulation for over a decade and these few had commonly borne a premium. Persons contracting debts, therefore, contemplated payment of them in United States silver coins or Spanish silver coins or in their equivalents in bank notes, and the legislation of 1834 and 1837 did not change the silver content of these coins. The act of 1837 also discontinued all coinage charges.

How the New Ratio Worked

From the enactment of the coinage laws of 1834 and 1837 to the suspension of specie payment at the end of 1861, our new mint ratio ruled above the world-market ratio and above the bimetallic ratio prevailing in France. After 1850, moreover, the greatly increased world production of gold resulting from the discoveries of gold in California and Australia increased this differential substantially.

With such an overvaluation of gold at our mint, it was inevitable that gold coinage should heavily predominate over silver coinage and that gold should tend strongly to drive silver out of circulation

[77]

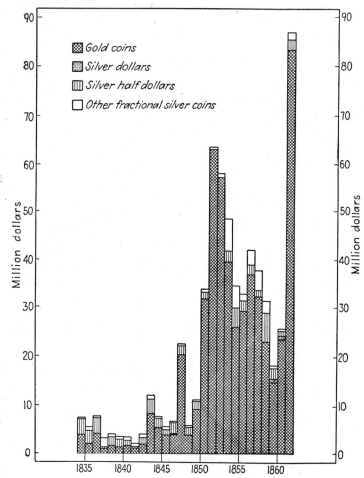

CHART 2.—Coinage of gold and silver at the United States Mint, 1834–1861.

—particularly, the larger silver coins, which were those least abraded and relatively the least expensive to collect. Chart 2 shows what happened from 1834 until the suspension of specie payments at the end of 1861.[1]

From 1834 to 1852 (the last complete year before fractional silver coins were made fiduciary), the total coinage of gold was $225 million and that of full-weight silver coins (*i.e.*, all silver coins except the three-cent pieces of 1851 and 1852)[2] was $41.2 million, making the gold coinage approximately $5.50 to each dollar of silver coinage. Although there was a considerable coinage of silver nearly every year from 1834 to 1850, after 1850 the coinage of full-weight silver coins became negligible. The great bulk of the silver coins minted during the years 1834 to 1852 were half dollars (as it had been prior to 1834). Out of a total silver coinage of $41,-200,000, during this period, silver dollars amounted to only $1,067,000. The coinage of quarters, dimes, and half dimes was much larger than during the preceding period.

Prior to 1850, the value ratio of gold to silver was not sufficiently below 16 to 1 to give a very large premium on silver coins—the premium having ruled most of the time in the neighborhood of 1 per cent. While this premium led to the rapid disappearance from circulation of the few silver dollars that were

---

[1] See KEMMERER, *op. cit.*, p. 352.
[2] *Cf.* pp. 81–82.

minted and of some of the half dollars, it was not sufficient to cover the cost of collecting and shipping fractional coins of denominations lower than fifty cents on any considerable scale and to yield a fair profit on the transaction. Down to about 1850, therefore, the supply of fractional silver money, although it was often not adequate, was still not deficient enough to cause the public serious inconvenience. Much of the fractional money, however, during those years was in bad condition.

Under the influence of the great flood of gold poured onto the world's markets from the newly discovered gold fields of California and Australia, the value ratio of gold to silver fell rapidly during the period 1848 to 1859, and this meant an increasing premium on silver coins. For example, while the ratio of 15.85 to 1, prevailing in 1848, was equivalent to a premium of 0.8 per cent on American silver coins, the ratio of 15.33, prevailing in 1853, was equivalent to a premium of 4.3 per cent. Not only did the receipts of silver at the mint fall off rapidly, but the silver in circulation began to disappear, at first the half dollars and then the smaller denominations. Everywhere the public were protesting against the scarcity of small change.

Various measures were adopted to meet the situation. In 1849 the government began to coin $1 gold pieces, and from then until 1862 it coined approximately $19 million of these pieces. In 1854, $3 gold pieces began to be minted and the coinage of two and a half dollar gold pieces was greatly increased after 1849. Bank notes for fractional parts of a dollar were put into circulation, also bank notes for odd amounts, such as $1.25, $1.50, and $1.75. There were, besides, privately issued notes and coins. In the country districts we find an increasing resort by the public to "sharp change" or "cut money," *viz.*, Spanish dollars cut into quarters, eighths, and sixteenths. Bank notes also were torn into halves and quarters, and these fractional parts of notes were popularly dubbed *rags*.

At this time there was introduced into circulation the 3-cent silver piece,[1] a coin of historical significance because it was the first American fiduciary, or token, silver coin. It was authorized by the act of March 3, 1851, which reduced the rate of letter postage in the United States from 5 cents to 3 cents. This 3-cent piece was to weigh $12\frac{3}{8}$ grains gross and to be 0.750 fine—all our other gold and silver coins, as previously noted, were 0.900 fine. This gave $33\frac{1}{3}$ 3-cent pieces the same gross weight as a dollar of our other silver coins, but a pure-silver content $16\frac{2}{3}$ per cent less. The difference was ample to protect the 3-cent piece from the melting pot and from exportation. Its legal-tender quality was limited to 30 cents, and it was, therefore, the first American silver coin to have its legal-tender quality limited.

England had permanently made her silver coins fiduciary money with limited legal tender in 1816,

[1] See CAROTHERS, *op. cit.*, pp. 108, 109, and 111.

and the matter of the desirability of our reducing the silver content of our fractional silver coins and treating them as subsidiary money had been discussed in official circles from time to time for at least a generation. A number of bills containing carefully worked-out plans to this effect had been at different times introduced in Congress. It was with the small beginning represented by this 3-cent piece, however, in 1851, motivated in part by a desire to have a coin of a denomination convenient for the purchase of postage stamps at the new letter rate, that fiduciary, or token, silver coinage was inaugurated in the United States. These 3-cent pieces were coined in large quantities during the years 1851 to 1853.

By 1853, the inconveniences to the public arising from the scarcity of fractional money had become so great that Congress was forced to take further action to provide the country with an adequate supply of coins for change. It did so by the law of February 21, 1853, which closed the mint to the free coinage of silver in fractional denominations, reduced the weight of all fractional silver coins (except the 3-cent piece), and limited the legal-tender quality of these coins to $5. The reduction in weight thus effected gave our silver coins a fine-silver content approximately 7.6 per cent less to the dollar than the silver dollar itself.[1]

---

[1] Ten days later, Congress changed the silver content of the 3-cent piece so as to bring it into conformity with that of our other fractional silver coins.

During the next 8 years the coinage of fractional silver coins was large and their reduced weights gave them adequate protection from the melting pot.[1]

By 1860, we had in the United States a generous supply of gold coin. We had got rid of our foreign coins and were well provided with fractional silver. At this juncture, however, the country found itself in the cataclysm of a civil war. The banks suspended specie payments on December 30, 1861, government legal-tender issues were soon resorted to, and both gold and silver coins were largely driven out of circulation, except in a few parts of the Far West, notably California and Oregon. The country was on a paper-money standard, the so-called *greenback* standard, until January 1, 1879. Then the resumption of specie payment placed the country firmly on a system of gold monometallism, *viz.*, the single gold standard, on the basis of a law enacted in 1873.

Since the subject of this book is gold money and

[1] From the Mint Act of 1792 until after the middle of the nineteenth century, Spanish and Mexican coins had continued in circulation. Although the circulation of Mexican dollars was now small, that of Spanish fractional coins of the denomination of 25 cents, 12½ cents, and 6¼ cents was still large. These coins continued to be a confusing element in our monetary system, and the problem of getting rid of them was a difficult one for the government. The problem was finally solved by an act of February 21, 1857, which removed the legal-tender quality from all foreign coins that still possessed it and provided new methods for the withdrawal of these coins from circulation. This act, coming at a time when our new fractional coins were being provided in abundance, soon drove the foreign coins into the Treasury, whence they were sent to the mint for recoinage into American money.

the gold standard, the history of the nation's 17 years with the greenback standard[1] will not be told.

BIMETALLISM LEGALLY DISCONTINUED IN 1873

In 1873 Congress carried through a much-needed revision and codification of our mint and coinage laws. This codification act, it should be emphasized, was passed in the greenback period, when there were in circulation very few silver coins and when the greenback dollar was worth only about 88 cents in terms of the gold or the silver dollar. Moreover, from 1806 through 1872, the total coinage of silver dollars had been only approximately $6.25 million. Of this sum, only $3.5 million had been coined since the suspension of specie payments in 1861, and nearly all these coins had been exported to the Orient in connection with our foreign trade. This meant that in 1873 the American public were not very familiar with the American silver dollar and took little or no interest in its domestic circulation. When, therefore, Congress in codifying our coinage laws omitted from the list of coins the standard silver dollar, the action aroused no public attention. It was looked upon merely as a legal acceptance of an existing fact.

The law meant, however, that the free coinage of silver was legally discontinued,[2] and, although the

---

[1] The reader interested in the history of the greenback standard will find it briefly narrated in Chap. XII of my book, *Money*.

[2] The law did provide for the coinage of a larger sized silver dollar (420 grains, as against 412½ grains in the standard silver dollar), called the *trade dollar* and intended for use in our Oriental trade. Its legal-tender quality was

nation continued to be on a *de facto* paper-money standard for 7 years longer, and although the standard silver dollar, like all the gold coins, retained the quality of being unlimited legal tender, it ceased to be standard money. In effect, therefore, legal bimetallism, which had existed since the Mint Act of 1792, was abolished and, when the nation returned to a specie basis, January 1, 1879, it found itself on a *de facto* monometallic gold standard, with gold as the only metal enjoying the privilege of free coinage.

In the meantime, France and the other members of the Latin union had given up bimetallism, and there no longer existed anywhere in the world a truly bimetallic standard.

Many bimetallists later argued that the dropping of the standard silver dollar from our list of coins in 1873 was a surreptitious and even fraudulent discontinuance of bimetallism, and they dubbed this action *the crime of* 1873. The evidence does not support this charge,[1] although it is no credit to the intelligence of Congress in monetary matters that its members should have enacted legislation of such important future consequences without realizing what they were doing.

---

limited to $5, like that of our fractional silver coins. The free-coinage privilege, which it was given in 1873, was taken from it 3 years later, as was likewise its legal-tender privilege. Most of these trade dollars were exported from the country, and those remaining were retired from circulation in 1887. See David K. Watson, *History of American Coinage*, Chap. XVII.

[1] See LAUGHLIN, J. LAWRENCE, *A History of Bimetallism in the United States*, pp. 92–105, and WATSON, *op. cit.*, Chaps. VIII and IX.

The Beginning of a De Facto Gold Standard

It has just been shown how the legislation of 1873, which discontinued the coinage of the little-known American silver dollar during the greenback-standard period, created a situation in which a return to a specie basis would place the country on the gold standard. Two years later the passage of the Resumption Act, to become effective January 1, 1879, by providing for the return of specie payments, implemented the coming metallic-money standard, which was to be gold monometallism.

The pertinent features of the Resumption Act were (1) a provision that, on and after January 1, 1879, the Secretary of the Treasury should "redeem, in coin, the United States legal-tender notes then outstanding on their presentation for redemption, at the office of the Assistant Treasurer of the United States in the City of New York, in sums of not less than fifty dollars . . . "; (2) a provision authorizing the Secretary of the Treasury, in order to provide the specie required for such redemption, "to use any surplus revenue, from time to time, in the Treasury, . . . and to issue, . . . at not less than par, in coin," certain kinds of United States bonds that had been authorized by previous legislation; (3) a provision imposing upon the Secretary of the Treasury the duty of withdrawing from circulation the greenbacks outstanding, in excess of $300 million,[1] to the amount of 80 per cent of the new issues of national bank notes.[2]

The Secretary, within the broad limits of the Resumption Act, was to work out plans for bringing about resumption on the scheduled date.

Obviously, under the law as passed and the conditions prevailing, the only form of specie in which resumption could be made was gold. Silver no longer enjoyed the free-coinage privilege and there was no silver money circulating that was unlimited legal tender. There was, moreover, comparatively little gold coin, and most of what was actually circulating was on the Pacific Coast. To obtain the gold coin required for resumption, therefore, the Secretary was forced to sell bonds abroad—a policy that brought on him much unmerited public criticism. John Sherman, when he became Secretary of the Treasury in 1877, under President Hayes, initiated a vigorous policy of accumulating gold reserves.

There was much public opposition to the Resumption Act, largely on the part of people who feared that it would unduly reduce the country's supply of

[1] In January, 1875, there were in circulation $382 million of greenbacks and $352 million of national bank notes.

[2] Inasmuch as the National Bank Law of that time required national banks in the principal cities to maintain a reserve of 25 per cent of lawful money against their national bank notes and required the banks in other cities to maintain a reserve of 15 per cent, it was reasoned that the above-mentioned 80 per cent limit would keep the net circulation of greenbacks and national bank notes combined about where it was.

money. Congress, ultimately forced by public opinion to make concessions to this inflationary sentiment, passed a law on May 31, 1878, prohibiting a further reduction in the greenback circulation. This gave the country a permanent greenback issue of $347 million, which it retains to this day.

Secretary Sherman believed that the lowest gold reserve consistent with safety with which the country would be able to resume specie payments, was 40 per cent, or about $138 million. By January 1, 1879, he had accumulated $133 million. About two-thirds of this came from the sale of bonds and one-third from surplus revenue. Under his strong policy, the gold value of the greenbacks slowly but surely advanced, and 2 weeks before January 1, when resumption began, they were quoted at par.

The Gold Standard in Operation, 1879 to 1914

For the 36 years from 1879 to the outbreak of the First World War, the American gold standard functioned well and in a normal way, except for some compromising silver legislation and for a considerable appreciation in the value of gold during the first half of the period. These difficulties will be considered briefly before we describe the otherwise satisfactory functioning of the new gold-standard system.

Declining Commodity Prices

From the early eighties until a few years before the end of the century, commodity prices in the

United States tended downward, as is shown by the following table:

PRICES IN THE UNITED STATES, 1879 TO 1900
1879 = 100

Year	Wholesale prices, Bureau of Labor Statistics	General prices,[1] Federal Reserve Bank, New York
1879	100	100
1880	112	107
1881	115	111
1882	121	114
1883	112	111
1884	103	107
1885	95	103
1886	91	101
1887	94	103
1888	96	106
1889	91	104
1890	92	106
1891	91	107
1892	85	104
1893	87	106
1894	77	101
1895	79	101
1896	76	100
1897	76	100
1898	79	100
1899	85	104
1900	91	107

[1] "General prices" covers a weighted composite of wholesale prices, retail prices, security prices, and rents. (See p. 191, note.)

This downward trend of commodity prices in the United States under the gold standard was paralleled by similar trends in other gold-standard countries, including England, Germany, and France. In the United States, moreover, it followed the long period

[89]

of falling prices (1865 to 1878) accompanying the deflating back to gold parity of our greenback standard. While commodity prices in gold-standard countries were thus tending downward, the price of silver was falling and the market gold-silver ratio, which for centuries had ruled in the neighborhood of from 14 to 1 to 16 to 1, rose from 15.93 to 1, in 1873, to 18.39 to 1, in 1879, and to 34.20 to 1, in 1897.

Bimetallists' Criticisms of Gold Standard

During about 20 years of political agitation on the money question, the bimetallists and others interested in silver stressed the evil effects of falling prices and blamed them largely on the discontinuance of bimetallism. They argued that the shift of many leading countries of the world to the gold standard from bimetallism since the early seventies had placed an increasingly heavy monetary demand on gold, while greatly decreasing the monetary demand for silver and destroying its erstwhile unlimited market at the mints. The resulting decline in commodity prices in gold-standard countries, they held, was having many harmful effects, among which they stressed the following.

Falling prices, so they said, meant an increasing value or purchasing power of the money unit in which all debts were payable, and this imposed a continually increasing burden upon the debtor classes, particularly the farmers, who were receiving progressively lower prices for their products and paying their mortgage debts in a dollar of ever-increasing value.

Continually falling prices, they further pointed out, exercised a depressing influence on business, causing unemployment and financial crises, and they argued that the readoption of bimetallism would, by bringing silver to the assistance of gold as a standard money metal, increase the money supply and thereby stop falling prices.

Another argument advanced by bimetallists against the substitution of gold monometallism for bimetallism was that it had broken down the so-called *nexus* between countries on different metallic money standards. As long as some countries were on a bimetallic standard, with the unlimited coinage of both gold and silver at a fixed mint ratio, the fluctuation would be very slight in the gold price of silver in gold-standard countries and in the silver price of gold in silver-standard countries. Foreign exchange rates, therefore, among countries on all three standards—bimetallic, gold, and silver—would be stable, as they were prior to 1873.

Since discontinuance of bimetallism, it was said, all this had been changed. The nexus between gold and silver was broken and each metal had gone its own way. There was thenceforth no limit to the possible variation in exchange rates between a gold-standard country and a silver-standard country. This brought a large new element of risk and speculation in foreign trade between countries on different metallic standards. It was an obstacle to the development of trade between gold- and silver-standard countries, as well as to the flow of funds for investment between such countries.

In Defense of the Gold Standard

The strongest arguments offered by the gold monometallists against the giving up of the gold standard and a return to bimetallism were the following: (1) Bimetallism had been tried in many countries for centuries and had always failed. As a result of such failures, it had been given up everywhere and, after 1874, there did not exist a single bimetallic country in the world. (2) No single country like the United States was strong enough alone to maintain a fixed gold-silver ratio as required by bimetallism, and this was overwhelmingly true for a low ratio like 16 to 1, then advocated by most bimetallists. The gold-standard advocates argued further that experience had shown that an effective agreement for international bimetallism on the part of a sufficient number of strong countries was politically impossible. (3) Silver was too bulky and inconvenient to be a standard metal under modern conditions. (4) Increased production of gold and increasing use of bank notes and bank-deposit currency, by economizing the use of gold, would soon stop the decline in prices—"the importance of which bimetallists greatly exaggerated." (5) The argument for bimetallism based on the need of a fixed par of exchange among gold- and silver-standard countries was rapidly losing its weight, by reason of the facts that most of the advanced countries of the world were already on a gold standard, while in most of the few remaining silver-standard countries there were strong movements in favor of the adoption of the gold standard.

In spite of many vigorous efforts to obtain an international bimetallic agreement among leading countries[1]—efforts extending over an entire generation and strongly favored by important interests in the leading countries of the world—no such agreement was ever obtained. Proposals such as that of William Jennings Bryan for national bimetallism never had much scientific standing anywhere.

"Doing Something for Silver"

Although the American gold standard held its own against advocates of a restoration of bimetallism, it was compelled to make concessions to "the silver group," a group consisting chiefly of international bimetallists, national bimetallists of the Bryan type, and people who had special interests in the silver industry itself, particularly in our half dozen principal silver-producing states.

The Bland-Allison Act. The first important concession to the silver group was the Bland-Allison Act, which was passed in 1878, shortly before the

[1] See RUSSELL, HENRY B., *International Monetary Conferences, Their Purpose, Character and Results.*

resumption of specie payments, and which was in operation until it was replaced by the Sherman Purchase Act of 1890.

For our purposes the kernel of the Bland-Allison Act was the provision for the coinage of standard silver dollars out of silver to be purchased at the market price by the Secretary of the Treasury in amounts of "not less than two million dollars' worth per month, nor more than four million dollars' worth per month, and cause the same to be coined monthly, as fast as so purchased, into such dollars . . . " Any holder of the silver dollars authorized by the act was permitted to deposit them with the Treasurer or any assistant treasurer of the United States and receive for them silver certificates of not less than $10 each. The coin deposited for or representing the certificates had to be retained in the Treasury for the redemption of the certificates, which were receivable for customs, taxes, and all public dues, and, when so received, might be reissued.

During the entire period in which the Bland-Allison Act was in operation, the Secretary of the Treasury, in the exercise of his option to buy not less than $2 million nor more than $4 million worth of silver each month, kept close to the minimum figure. Throughout the period, however, despite the artificial demands for silver created by these purchases, the gold price of silver declined almost continually. For the years 1878 to 1889, inclusive, the coinage of standard silver dollars amounted to $345 million. These silver dollars, however, were not popular in most parts of the country. The public, finding them cumbersome and inconvenient, called them *cart wheels*. They accumulated in the banks, and the public returned them in large quantities to the government in the payment of taxes and other government dues.

Their circulation "by proxy" was facilitated by the use of silver certificates, particularly those of the lower denominations, which were authorized by the law of 1886. By July 1, 1890, the circulation of silver dollars was only $56 million, while that of the certificates was $298 million.

In a personal letter to James A. Garfield, under date of July 19, 1880, Secretary Sherman said, "The silver law threatens to produce within a year or so a single silver standard . . . I could at any moment, by issuing silver freely, bring a crisis."[1]

The Sherman Purchase Act of 1890. During the later eighties, interest in the silver purchases under the Bland-Allison Act was quiescent, since the new silver certificates that were being put into circulation were for a time readily absorbed, thanks to the business prosperity and to a declining national bank-note circulation. However, William Windom, President Harrison's first Secretary of the Treasury, unexpectedly pushed the subject prominently into public attention by recommending in his first annual report to the President a new silver-coinage plan supplementing the Bland-Allison Act, which he

[1] Quoted by A. D. Noyes in *Forty Years of American Finance*, p. 74.

wished to have continued. Although this plan was never adopted, it became the basis of the Sherman Silver Purchase Act of 1890, which in that year replaced the Bland-Allison Act.

The new act was a compromise between the demands of the extreme bimetallists and those of the gold monometallists. The three principal provisions of this act were: (1) The Secretary of the Treasury was required to purchase silver bullion to the amount of 4,500,000 ounces each month, or such part of that sum as might be offered at a price not greater than $1 for the amount of silver contained in a silver dollar, *i.e.*, about 77 per cent of an ounce; and to pay for the silver so bought by the issuance of a new kind of money called *treasury notes*. It will be observed that when the price of silver declined the volume of treasury notes issued also declined, and when it rose the volume of treasury notes increased; whereas, under the Bland-Allison Act, which required the monthly purchase of not less than $2 million worth of silver nor more than $4 million worth, when the price of silver declined the amount of silver purchased for coinage into silver dollars rose, and when the price rose the volume purchased declined. (2) The treasury notes were made "redeemable on demand, in coin," and the law provided that, when so redeemed, they might be reissued. The redemption provision of the law is noteworthy in the light of subsequent developments. It was that upon demand of the holder of any of the Treasury notes herein provided for the Secretary of the Treasury shall, under such regulations as he may prescribe, redeem such notes in gold or silver coin, at his discretion, it being the established policy of the United States to maintain the two metals on a parity with each other upon the present legal ratio, or such ratio as may be provided by law.

(3) Unlike the silver certificates of the Bland-Allison Act, the treasury notes were made unlimited legal tender.

From the enactment of the Sherman law in July, 1890, to its repeal in October, 1894, the government bought 169 million ounces of silver, in payment for which it issued $156 million treasury notes.

During most of this time, the United States and a great part of Europe were suffering from a business depression. It was not a time in which the country could easily absorb substantial increases in its monetary circulation. The public, which was skeptical about the soundness of these new treasury notes— backed, as they were, by silver that had been depreciating for years in terms of gold—discriminated against them in favor of gold. In other words, in accordance with Gresham's law, the public held back the better money and passed on to others the poorer money. Furthermore, as money became relatively redundant through the pumping into circulation of these huge supplies of treasury notes, foreign-exchange rates advanced to the gold-export point, and gold, which had a good foreign market, went abroad, while American fiduciary money, including the treasury notes, stayed at home.

According to Dewey,[1]

> Before the passage of the Sherman Act nine-tenths or more of the customs receipts at the New York custom house were paid in gold and gold certificates; in the summer of 1891 the proportion of gold and gold certificates fell as low as 12 per cent; and in September, 1892, to less than 4 per cent. The use of United States notes and treasury notes of 1890 correspondingly increased.

The Sherman Purchase Act, it will be recalled, required the Secretary of the Treasury to redeem the treasury notes "in gold or silver coin at his discretion." The Secretary, however, always redeemed the notes, as he was legally obliged to redeem the United States notes, on demand in gold. For the first 4 months of 1893, redemption amounted to over $50 million, as compared with less than $2¼ million in the corresponding months of 1892. By April, 1893, the gold reserve in the Treasury had fallen below the conventional $100 million limit. The number of commercial failures in the country increased 50 per cent in 1893 over the preceding year, and the total liabilities were three times as large as in 1892. The situation became so bad that the businessmen of the country began to urge strongly the calling of a special session of Congress for the purpose of repealing the Sherman Purchase Act.

[1] DEWEY, DAVIS R., *Financial History of the United States*, pp. 443–444.

President Cleveland, who during his previous administration had been a strong opponent of the heavy coinage of silver required by the Bland-Allison Act, was from the beginning of his second administration also outspoken in his opposition to the Sherman Purchase Act. On June 30, 1893, 4 days after the closing of the Indian mints to the free coinage of silver, he called for an extraordinary session of Congress, to be convened on August 7. The day after Congress opened, he sent to it a vigorous call for the repeal of the Sherman Purchase Act and for other legislation that would "put beyond all doubt or mistake the intention and the ability of the Government to fulfill its pecuniary obligations in money universally recognized by all civilized countries." In explaining the breakdown of confidence resulting from the heavy silver purchases, he said:

Between the 1st day of July, 1890, and the 15th day of July, 1893, the gold coin and bullion in our Treasury decreased more than $132,000,000, while during the same period the silver coin and bullion in the Treasury increased more than $147,000,-000. Unless Government bonds are to be constantly sold to replenish our exhausted gold, only to be again exhausted, it is apparent that the operation of the silver purchase law leads in the direction of the entire substitution of silver for gold in the Government Treasury, and that this must be followed by the payment of all Government obligations in depreciated silver.

This, he pointed out, would constitute an abandonment of the gold standard.

[99]

The fight for repeal of the Sherman Purchase Act was a hard one, but the President won, and on October 30, 1893, the repeal law was passed. Not until 2 years later, however, and after four bond issues had been made by the government to maintain the gold standard through continually replenishing the gold reserve, and not until after the second defeat of William Jennings Bryan for the presidency on the issue of "16 to 1 national bimetallism," did the nation emerge from the crisis and find its gold standard again secure.

The Gold Standard Act of 1900

This security was clinched by the Gold Standard Act of 1900, which provided a definitive legal recognition and a further implementation of a gold standard that had been in operation since January 1, 1879.

There were two important provisions of this act, *viz.*, that

[1] the dollar consisting of twenty-five and eight-tenths grains of gold, nine-tenths fine . . . shall be the standard unit of value, and all forms of money issued or coined by the United States shall be maintained at a parity of value with this standard, and it shall be the duty of the Secretary of the Treasury to maintain such parity. . . . [2] United States notes, and Treasury notes . . . when presented to the Treasury for redemption, shall be redeemed in gold coin, . . . and in order to secure the prompt and certain redemption of such notes as herein provided it shall be the duty of the Secretary of the Treasury to set apart in the Treasury a reserve fund of one

hundred and fifty million dollars in gold coin and bullion, which fund shall be used for such redemption purposes only, and whenever and as often as any of said notes shall be redeemed from said fund it shall be the duty of the Secretary of the Treasury to use said notes so redeemed to restore and maintain such reserve fund . . .

Aside from the long but successful struggle with silver that the American gold standard waged for its existence during the first half of its life prior to 1914, and aside from the appreciation of gold during this period, the outstanding facts of the gold-standard period may be described in a few words. There was a moderate depreciation in the value of gold from 1896 to 1914, expressed in corresponding advances in commodity prices. This depreciation was due in part to (1) the rapid expansion of bank-deposit and bank-note currency, which served as substitutes for gold in hand-to-hand circulation and as a mechanism for making existing gold supplies more efficient, and to (2) the great increase in the world's supply of monetary gold coming chiefly from the newly discovered gold deposits in South Africa. Between 1896 and 1914, the world's reported annual production of gold increased from $203 million to $408 million, or by 101 per cent. During the same 18 years, in the United States, wholesale commodity prices rose 46 per cent and general prices rose 41 per cent.

Throughout these years of gold-standard orthodoxy the coinage of gold at American mints was both

[101]

free and gratuitous. Anyone could take gold to the mints and obtain in exchange its full value in gold coins, without charge for the process of coinage, and be held only for charges adequate to cover the expenses incurred in the "refining and partage" of the bullion.

From 1879 to 1914, gold was coined in substantial quantities every year, the total for the period by denominations having been as follows:

COINAGE OF GOLD AT UNITED STATES MINTS, 1879 TO 1914[1]

Denomination	Amount	Percentage
$20	$2,537,977,000	69.00
10	472,658,000	12.79
5	661,495,000	17.78
3	72,402	
2.50	15,059,692	0.41
1	818,312	0.02
	$3,678,080,406	100.00

[1] Computed from annual data given in the Director of the Mint's *Annual Report*, 1942, p. 69.

Throughout the period, the exportation and importation of gold were free of tariff and other trade restrictions in the United States, and every year there was a substantial movement of gold in both directions. Gold always enjoyed the privileges of being unlimited legal tender and acceptable for all taxes and other government dues. In practice, all other kinds of lawful money, both notes and coins, usually were easily exchangeable for gold at par.

Gold money circulated to a considerable extent in the form of gold certificates, or "yellowbacks," which originated with a law of 1863, authorizing the Secretary of the Treasury to issue them against deposits at par of gold coin and bullion, the gold so deposited for or representing the certificates to be retained 100 per cent in the Treasury for the payment of the certificates on demand. While the certificates were true money and circulated freely, they partook of the nature of warehouse receipts. The gold belonged to the owner of the certificate and "it circulated by proxy" in the form of the certificate. During this period, gold certificates were not legal tender. Their circulation amounted to about $15 million in 1879, $131 million in 1890, $201 million in 1900, and $1,026 million in 1914.

The unit of value, as we have seen, was the gold dollar containing 23.22 grains of pure gold. Inasmuch as there are 480 grains of gold in an ounce, an ounce of gold could be coined into $20.67 of United States gold coin. Since we had free coinage of gold, anyone could take pure gold bullion in any quantity to an American mint and have it minted into gold coin, receiving for each ounce $20.67 (less certain petty charges for assaying, refining, partage, etc.,), while anyone melting down American gold coins of full weight could get an ounce of pure gold out of every $20.67 worth of gold coin melted. Thus in the United States at that time, to say that an ounce of gold was worth $20.67 was like saying that a foot was 12 inches long; $20.67 was, in reality, an ounce of pure gold put up in the form of money.

There were in circulation in the country in 1914 about $3.4 billion of money, of which about $1.6 billion consisted of gold and gold certificates, while the balance consisted of various kinds of paper money and of coins of silver, nickel, and copper, which the national government was obliged to maintain at a parity with gold. About 90 per cent, however, of the country's total business, amounting to many hundreds of billions of dollars annually, was performed by bank deposits circulating by means of bank checks, "deposit currency." Yet the value of every dollar of our paper currency, the value of all our coins, and the value of our enormous volume of deposit currency were expressed in terms of the value of a gold dollar, *viz.*, the value of 23.22 grains of gold. Anything that affected the value of gold in the world's gold market affected the value of the gold dollar, in which this tremendous amount of business was being done and in terms of which all our prices, wages, and debts were expressed and paid.

SELECTED BIBLIOGRAPHY

ANDREW, A. PIATT: *Statistics for the United States* 1867–1909, National Monetary Commission, Government Printing Office, Washington, D.C., 1910.

BRUCE, P. A.: *Economic History of Virginia*, The Macmillan Company, New York, 1907.

BULLOCK, CHARLES J.: *Essays on the Monetary History of the United States*, The Macmillan Company, New York, 1900.

CHALMERS, ROBERT: *A History of Currency in the British Colonies*, Eyre and Spottiswoode, London, 1893.

CAROTHERS, NEIL: *Fractional Money*, John Wiley & Sons, Inc., New York, 1930.

CROSBY, S. S.: *Early Coins of America*, Estes and Lauriat, Boston, 1878.

DAVIS, A. M.: *Currency and Banking in the Province of Massachusetts Bay*, American Economic Association, Evanston, Ill., 1901.

DEL MAR, A.: *A History of the Precious Metals*, George Bell and Sons, London, 1880.

DE KNIGHT, WILLIAM F.: *History of the Currency of the Country and of the Loans of the United States from the Earliest Period to June* 30, 1900, Government Printing Office, Washington, D.C., 1900.

Director of the Mint: *Annual Reports*, Government Printing Office, Washington, D.C., *passim*.

DEWEY, DAVIS R.: *Financial History of the United States*, 10th ed., Longmans, Green and Company, New York, 1928.

EVANS, GEORGE G.: *Illustrated History of the United States Mint*, George G. Evans, Philadelphia, 1891.

FELT, J. B.: *An Historical Account of Massachusetts Currency*, Perkins and Marvin, Boston, 1839.

HICKCOX, J. H.: *Historical Account of American Coinage*, Author, Albany, N. Y., 1858.

International Monetary Conference: held in Paris in August, 1878 . . . *Senate Eexcutive Document* 58, Forty-fifth Congress, Third Session, Government Printing Office, Washington, D.C., 1879.

————: held at Brussels in 1892, Government Printing Office, Washington, D.C., 1893.

KEMMERER, EDWIN WALTER: *Money—The Principles of Money and Their Exemplification in Outstanding Chapters of Monetary History*, The Macmillan Company, New York, 1935.

Monetary Commission of the Indianapolis Convention: *Report*, University of Chicago Press, Chicago, 1898.

LAUGHLIN, J. LAWRENCE: *A History of Bimetallism in the United States*, D. Appleton-Century Company, Inc., New York, 1881.

MITCHELL, WESLEY CLAIR: *Gold, Prices, and Wages under the Greenback Standard*, University of California Press, Berkeley, 1908.

———: *A History of Greenbacks*, University of Chicago Press, Chicago, 1903.

MOSES, BERNARD: Legal Tender Notes in California, *Quarterly Journal of Economics*, vol. VII, 1893.

NOYES, A. D.: *Forty Years of American Finance*, G. P. Putnam's Sons, (Knickerbocker Press), New York, 1909.

RUSSELL, HENRY B.: *International Monetary Conferences, Their Purpose, Character and Results*, Harper & Brothers, New York, 1898.

STEWART, F. H.: *History of the First United States Mint*, privately printed, Camden, N. J., 1924.

SUMNER, WILLIAM GRAHAM: *A History of American Currency*, Henry Holt and Company, Inc., New York, 1874.

———: The Spanish Dollar and the Colonial Shilling, *American Historical Review*, vol. III, 1898.

WALKER, FRANCIS A.: *Discussions in Economics and Statistics*, ed. by Davis R. Dewey, 2 vols., Henry Holt and Company, Inc., New York, 1899.

———: *International Bimetallism*, Henry Holt and Company, Inc., New York, 1897.

WATSON, DAVID K.: *History of American Coinage*, G. P. Putnam's Sons (Knickerbocker Press), New York, 1899.

WHITE, HORACE: *Money and Banking*, 5th ed., Ginn and Company, Boston, 1914.

YOUNG, JOHN PARKE: *European Currency and Finance*, 2 vols., Government Printing Office, Washington, D.C., 1925.

CHAPTER IV

The Breakdown of the International Gold Standard— Its Recovery and Relapse

C'est la guerre.—ANONYMOUS.

For about four-fifths of the time included in the 30 years of gold-standard history reviewed in this chapter, most of the world was on a paper-money standard. The only two important nations that stand as exceptions to this statement are China, in which the silver standard ruled for about two-thirds of the time and the paper-money standard for the other third, and the United States, in which the gold standard prevailed for about 90 per cent of the time. Only for approximately a half dozen years, ending in the early thirties, was the large majority of the leading countries of the world on the gold standard. Inasmuch as the subject of this book is gold money and the gold standard, the recent experiences with paper-money standards, important though they are for all students of money, will not be discussed here.

THE INTERNATIONAL MONETARY SITUATION FOLLOWING THE OUTBREAK OF THE FIRST WORLD WAR

At the outbreak of war in 1914, there were 59 countries classified by the United States Bureau of the Mint as on the gold standard (including the gold-exchange standard).[1] They included practically all of Europe, most of Asia except China, all of North America except Mexico, and a large part of South America, including three of the four principal countries. China was at the time seriously considering the introduction of the gold standard and Mexico had only lapsed from the gold standard briefly in a period of revolution.

Then, under the stress of a world war, the gold standard was practically driven off the map within the brief period of 2 or 3 years. The last important country to abandon it was the United States, which in 1917 placed an embargo on the exportation of gold. Not only did practically all gold standards break down during the 10 years of war and reconstruction, but all the scores of countries that resorted to paper-money standards suffered very serious inflation. In some belligerent countries—like Germany, Russia, and Poland—prices rose to astronomical heights. In others the inflation, though severe, was not astronomical; for example, in France, Belgium, and Italy price advances reached magnitudes of the order of 300 to 600 per cent. In some other countries inflation, although real, was of still lower magnitude. In England, for example, between 1914 and 1920 the wholesale price level rose 195 per cent; in Norway from January, 1915, to December, 1920, 128 per cent, and in the United States from September, 1917,

---

[1] *Monetary Systems of the Principal Countries of the World*, 1916, pp. 3 and 4.

to the end of June, 1919—the brief period of 21 months of the gold embargo—wholesale prices rose 10 per cent.

With few exceptions, the paper-money standards of the war and early postwar period were terrible failures. In the field of economics, the war probably left no conviction stronger with the masses of the people of Europe than that *never again* did they want to suffer the evils of such an orgy of inflated paper money. Everywhere there was a popular longing to get back to a "solid" monetary standard, to something in which the people had confidence; and in the distracted world of that time there was no other commodity in which they had so much confidence as gold.

Public Sentiment Strong for a Return to Gold

Accordingly, in every part of the world plans were discussed and measures taken looking toward an early return to the international gold standard. It was a striking fact that in these early postwar years there was almost no public agitation for any other kind of monetary standard than gold.

The International Financial Conference held at Brussels in 1920, at which all the important nations of the world—39 in number—were represented, resolved unanimously: "It is highly desirable that the countries which have lapsed from an effective gold standard should return thereto . . . " Two years later, the International Economic Conference held at Genoa declared:

> An essential requisite for the economic reconstruction of Europe is the achievement by each country of stability in the value of its currency. . . . Measures of currency reform will be facilitated if the practice of continuous cooperation among central banks can be developed. . . . It is desirable that all European currencies should be based upon a common standard. . . . Gold is the only common standard which all European countries could at present agree to adopt. . . . In a number of countries it will not be possible for some years to restore an effective gold standard; but it is in the general interest that the European Governments should declare now that this is their ultimate object, and should agree on the programme by way of which they intend to achieve it.

Such, in a few words, was the situation when the postwar world began its trek back to the gold standard.

THE RETURN TO GOLD

With the removal of the gold-export embargo in June, 1919, the United States became the first country, after the war, to return to the gold standard. Inasmuch as its departure from gold had been not only brief but also slight, and inasmuch as during that period considerable gold coin had continued to circulate within the country, at parity with other money, the return was without disturbing consequences.[1] During the next 8 years most of the

[1] There was no coinage of gold (except a few memorial dollar pieces) at American mints during the 3 years, 1917–1919.

other countries of the world returned to the gold standard, and by 1927 the number of gold-standard countries was greater than ever before.

Rates of Stabilization

One of the most controversial monetary subjects during these years of the return to gold was the rate of stabilization, *i.e.*, the question of the proper gold content for the new monetary unit in each country, including the question of the rate at which the existing depreciated paper money should be made convertible into this new unit. This problem was one that had to be solved in scores of countries, and the literature concerning it, both official and unofficial, is voluminous. A detailed discussion does not fall within the scope of this book, but it will be useful to consider very briefly a few of the more important phases of the problem.

For many countries whose currencies had become badly depreciated, it was out of the question to return to the prewar gold parity. That would have involved a tragic deflation. For such countries the only course was to stabilize at a gold monetary unit that would represent the approximate current value (or an easy multiple thereof) of the existing paper-money unit. It was a question of giving prices and exchange rates an opportunity "to settle down to normal equilibrium" (or "purchasing power parity") and of then stabilizing at or near that value.

This, broadly speaking, was the policy adopted

by most of these countries, of which the following are typical examples. France stabilized at approximately 5 to 1, making its paper franc equivalent to a new gold franc having a pure-gold content approximately equal to one-fifth that of the old gold franc (Act of June 25, 1928). Belgium stabilized at about 7 to 1, making her paper franc equivalent to a new gold franc having a pure-gold content equal to 14.4 per cent of that of its prewar franc (Royal Decree, October 25, 1926). Italy stabilized at approximately 3.7 to 1, making her paper lira equivalent to a new gold lira containing approximately 27.3 per cent as much gold as the prewar lira. Greece stabilized with a new gold drachma representing a stabilization rate of approximately 15 to 1. Austria created a new gold monetary unit equal in gold value to about 14 cents in United States money of that time, and then made her paper money convertible into this unit at the rate of 10,000 to 1. Poland followed a course similar to that of Austria, but its conversion rate was 1,300,000 to 1. Germany stabilized at a trillion paper marks to one new gold reichsmark, which had the same gold content as the prewar mark.

For countries in which the depreciation of the paper-money unit in terms of gold had been small— e.g., the United States, Canada, Switzerland, Greece, Argentina, and Venezuela—the case for stabilization at the prewar gold parity was a fairly clear one and this was the plan they adopted.

For the intermediate countries, in which for a

considerable time the currency had been at a substantial but moderate discount in terms of the prewar gold unit, the problem was a more difficult one. Should they deflate back to gold parity or stabilize near the *status quo?* In this group were to be found the United Kingdom, Australia, the Union of South Africa, the Netherlands, Norway, Denmark, and a number of other countries.

The principal arguments in favor of deflating back to the prewar gold parity were as follows: (1) It was the highly ethical thing to do. Debts both public and private would then be payable in the long-standing, legal monetary unit of the country, in terms of which the prewar debts still outstanding had been contracted. (2) It would maintain and perhaps even strengthen the country's prestige in the world of finance. Take, for example, the case of Great Britain's gold pound sterling, which had been maintained without debasement for nearly a century, and had become the international unit of account and settlement not only for a large "sterling area," but also for much of the rest of the world. The pound had an international prestige that was clearly well worth making a sacrifice to maintain. (3) It would permit the continued use of the money then in circulation and the restoration to the circulation of the specie held in hoards[1] at home and in

---

[1] For an instructive episode in Mexico of the war period, involving a widespread restoration of hoarded gold coin to circulation after a long period of inflation, see Edwin Walter Kemmerer, *Inflation and Revolution*, pp. 114–118.

hiding abroad; and thereby both public convenience and economy would be served.

The return of prewar gold parity was widely favored also for selfish reasons by special interests that expected to benefit thereby, such as, (1) creditors, who would be paid in a more valuable monetary unit if the old gold parity should be restored; (2) importers, who presumably would temporarily benefit by increasing the purchasing power abroad of the home monetary unit; and (3) certain groups of organized labor, whose wages had risen as wartime inflation had progressed, and who felt themselves to be strong enough to resist wage reductions as the cost of living should fall, under a national program of deflation.

The arguments advanced in favor of stabilizing at or near the existing gold value of the monetary unit, which were naturally, to a large degree, merely the other side of the shield, included the following: (1) Deflation, with its long period of falling prices and its heavy downward pressure on wages, would be disturbing to the economic life of the nation, causing business depressions, unemployment, and business failures. (2) Such a deflation program would penalize the debtor classes for the benefit of the creditor classes. (3) While temporarily stimulating the country's import trade, deflation would also temporarily raise in terms of foreign moneys the prices of the country's exports and thereby depress production for export. (4) The advocates of stabilization at the *status quo* answered the "ethical" argument of their opponents by saying that a large part of the debt outstanding at the time had been incurred in depreciated paper money since the outbreak of the war, and that it would be unethical to compel a man who, under stress of war, borrowed depreciated paper money to repay his debts in a gold-standard unit of greater value.

The nation's export trade, the *status quo* advocates argued, would be in a stronger position if stabilization were effected at the prevailing value, because foreign importers could buy the country's goods on better terms if its monetary unit were cheap than if it were dear in terms of their own money. Under deflation, it was said, the foreign-exchange value of the local money unit would rise more rapidly than export-commodity prices would fall.

In most countries of this intermediate group, of which Great Britain was the outstanding example, stabilization was effected by a return through a process of deflation to prewar gold parity.

Regardless of the merits and demerits of the two sides of the controversy as a whole, there is no question but that many economic hardships experienced during the twenties in these countries, and particularly in Great Britain, were attributable in a high degree to the policy of deflating to prewar gold parity.

The Gold Standard of the Twenties

In a brief survey of the restored gold standard of the twenties, the three most important facts to be noted are (1) the war-weakened and distorted economic milieu in which the restored gold standard had to function, (2) the changed and debilitated character of the new gold standard itself, and (3) the brief period of its operation. These three considerations will be discussed in the paragraphs that follow.

The Changed Economic Milieu

The new gold standard was required to function in a different environment, one that was much less favorable than that of the prewar gold standard. Among important changes for the worse may be cited the following: (1) the destruction that had been wrought by the greatest war in history—a destruction of scores of billions of dollars of property and of over 13 million lives, representing much of the best blood of the world, the blood of men who, if they had lived, would have been in the prime of life during these years; (2) the great maladjustments in the production of various basic commodities after the war, growing out of the efforts of different countries during the war to produce goods for themselves which war conditions prevented them from importing as formerly, or to produce certain classes of goods in greater volume for war needs. These created dangerous and uneconomic vested

[116]

interests for the postwar period. They contributed to excess stocks of various commodities, reduced to a lower level than would otherwise have existed the efficiency of world economic production and distribution, and were an important factor in the great decline that occurred in the world's international trade; (3) the tremendous redistribution of wealth that was caused by the inflation, with its resulting injustices, economic hardships, political resentments, and decreased capital efficiency; (4) the large and increasing amount of restriction placed on international trade in the form of higher tariffs, quotas, exchange restrictions, currency depreciation, antidumping regulations, arbitrary customs valuations and rulings, so-called *trade-clearing agreements*, and the like. Many of these restrictions were the results of efforts to maintain uneconomic industry, expanded production in specified lines, or unduly high wage scales, created by the abnormal conditions existing during the war. They represented wasteful efforts to resist the natural economic liquidation of the war; (5) the large backwash of basic commodities that the world accumulated by reason of its attempt to defy the law of demand and supply, through valorization schemes intended to hold up prices without controlling the supply of the products. Examples were rubber, coffee, copper, wheat, and sugar; (6) the burden of interallied debt obligations and particularly the uncertainty and tension that grew out of attempts to solve the problem of war debts.

[117]

A Changed and Weakened Gold Standard

Not only did the postwar gold standard have to function in a much less congenial milieu than did that of the prewar days, but the standard itself was of a weaker type. The three principal causes of this weakness were these:

A Gold-bullion and Gold-exchange Standard Superseding the Gold-coin Standard. Outside the United States and a few minor countries, the predominately ante bellum gold-coin standard, with its free coinage of gold and full convertibility of fiduciary money into gold coin on demand, gave way to the gold-bullion standard and the gold-exchange standard.[1] In both cases, the minting and circulation of gold coin were usually nonexistent, and in both it became difficult for people of small means to obtain monetary gold. Under these new-type standards, the hoarding of gold, which creates a varying demand for the yellow metal and often serves as a check against inflationary forces, was rendered difficult for the masses of the people.

A Postwar Gold Standard That Was Subjected to More Managing. The postwar gold standard nearly everywhere was less automatic in its functioning than was the prewar standard. Under the gold-

---

[1] Under the gold-bullion standard, redemption was usually only in gold bars of large denomination; and under the gold-exchange standard, redemption was entirely or chiefly in gold drafts of large denomination drawn on a reserve fund deposited in some financial center or centers outside the country. See pp. 152–160 and 174–176.

bullion and gold-exchange standards it became easier for governments and central banks to manipulate the currency supply and to "slip away from the gold points" than it was under a gold-coin standard, with gold in circulation and gold-coin convertibility. Government management of economic affairs, which had reached new heights during the war emergency, persisted long after that emergency had passed. This was particularly true in the field of money. Directly and through central banks, which they increasingly controlled, governments managed their currencies on a large scale. Central banks no longer depended for their monetary and credit controls chiefly upon modest manipulation of discount rates and occasional minor operations in the open market, but resorted extensively to large open-market operations, the exercise of foreign-exchange control, and the manipulation of reserve requirements. Some of this management was scientific and useful, while some was political or otherwise harmful. Natural checks and balances of economic forces were all too often interfered with by ignorant meddlers. Normal economic forces were sidetracked before they were given a chance to correct evils. It was not so much a question of management or no management as one of too much management and too many incompetent managers.

Inadequate Gold Reserves. In the third place, most countries that returned to the gold standard during the later twenties did so with inadequate gold reserves, which they obtained in large part by borrowing from abroad.

The Brief Life of the Postwar Gold Standard

The final outcome was that, before the new gold standard could be perfected and firmly established, it was destroyed by the world economic crisis of the early thirties. Every country that returned to the gold standard after the war and a few that had established the gold standard *de novo* gave it up during the years 1929 to 1936. It is often difficult to fix the exact date at which a country actually gave up the gold standard, because the date of the *de jure* departure from gold was usually later than that of the *de facto* departure; while the latter, which is the more important, was commonly not a *jump* but a *slide*. Among the 59 countries that went off the gold standard between 1929 and 1936, 20 of the more important are listed here, approximately in their chronological order.[1]

	1929
Argentine	December
Austria	December
Uruguay	December
	1931
Brazil	March
Germany	July
United Kingdom	September

[1] See League of Nations, *Monetary Review*, 1937, p. 111.

India	September
Norway	September
Denmark	September
Sweden	September
Canada	October
Japan	December
1932	
Chile	April
Peru	May
1933	
United States	March
1934	
Italy	May
1935	
Belgium	March
1936	
Poland	April
France	September
Netherlands	September

The Gold Standard in the United States since 1929

The fundamental reasons for the universal breakdown of the postwar gold standard have been briefly summarized, and the limits of this book preclude a discussion of the special situations in the different countries. Inasmuch, however, as the United States soon returned to a gold standard, and as we shall presently describe this new type of gold-bullion standard, it will be useful at this point to review

briefly the events in the United States that led up
to its establishment.

Events Leading to a New Type of Gold Standard

In the United States during the early years of the
world economic depression the position of the gold
standard was strong. For a number of years we had
experienced a heavy net importation of gold and in
consequence we possessed a superabundance of the
yellow metal. Despite a highly speculative boom in
the security markets during the years immediately
preceding the crash of 1929, we had had in this
country over a period of about 8 years one of the
most stable commodity price levels we ever experienced.[1] In August, 1931, the month before Great
Britain went off the gold standard, our American
stock of monetary gold was $4.6 billion, the highest
in our history up to that date. By January, 1933,
this stock had declined to $4.1 billion, but was still
by far the largest stock of monetary gold in the
world and constituted one-third of the world's total
known supply.

Then suddenly we were confronted with the events
that culminated in the "bank holiday" of early
March, 1933. There were widespread runs on our
banks, a great break of confidence in the currency,
and a pronounced hoarding movement, which was
unique in that it involved the hoarding of unusual

---

[1] KEMMERER, EDWIN WALTER, Gold and the Gold Standard, *Proceedings of
the American Philosophical Society*, vol. LXXI, No. 3 (1932), pp. 87–102.

amounts of gold as contrasted with paper currency. This breakdown in the public's confidence in its money and banking system was due largely to the rapidly growing fear of the cheap-money policies that were being strongly urged by men in high places, both in Congress and outside, to the failure of Roosevelt, in contrast with President Hoover, to take a strong stand for sound money in the election campaign and between his election and his inauguration,[1] and to the widespread and persistent rumors immediately following the election, that the president-elect was giving a ready ear to the advocates of dollar devaluation and other radical monetary policies.

Had Roosevelt, immediately after his election, joined President Hoover in a bipartisan declaration, of the ringing, Grover Cleveland type, that the gold standard and the existing gold dollar would be maintained at all hazards and that, to this end, all the financial resources of the United States would be mobilized if necessary, such a declaration, coupled with a reasonable policy of party cooperation, would probably have prevented the disastrous collapse of our currency and banking system in early 1933. In that case the breakdown of the American gold standard with its subsequent devaluation of the dollar would have been avoided.

[1] See CRAWFORD, ARTHUR WHIPPLE, *Monetary Management under the New Deal*, Chap. II; William Starr Myers, and Walter H. Newton, *The Hoover Administration*, pp. 297–300 and Chaps. XVIII and XIX; and Ray Lyman Wilbur and Arthur Mastick Hyde, *The Hoover Policies*, pp. 470–475.

However, confronted with the situation as it existed at the time of his inauguration, the President and his associates handled the banking crisis wisely during March and the forepart of April. As an emergency measure, the Banking Act of March 9, 1933, was in most respects sound, as was also its early administration.

By March 4, 1933, the banks in almost all the states were either closed or operating under strong government restrictions. It was temporarily difficult for the public to obtain money, and from then on it was practically impossible for it to obtain gold coin. On March 6, the President issued his proclamation declaring a "bank holiday" and effectively suspending the gold standard. Three days later, the emergency banking bill became law.[1]

The response of the country to these vigorous emergency measures was prompt. Between March 4 and April 4, $1,225,000,000 of money returned to the

---

[1] The act gave the President "during time of war or during any other period of national emergency" practically unlimited power to regulate and control foreign-exchange operations, credit transfers and payments, and the "export, hoarding, melting, or earmarking of the coin or bullion." It also gave him authority, which he promptly exercised, to require the public "to pay and deliver to the Treasurer of the United States any or all gold coin, gold bullion, and gold certificates" owned by anyone, payment therefor to be made in "an equivalent amount of any other form of coin or currency coined or issued under the laws of the United States."

The law further provided that during the emergency "no member bank of the Federal Reserve system, shall transact any banking business except to such extent and subject to such regulations . . . as may be prescribed by the Secretary of the Treasury with the approval of the President." The law provided methods by which the Government throughout the emergency could aid and administer banks that were in difficulty.

reserve banks and the ratio of reserves to Federal Reserve notes and deposits combined advanced from 45 to 60 per cent. Funds arising out of this return flow of currency,

were used by the member banks to reduce their borrowing at the Reserve banks by $1,000,000,000 and in addition to reduce the acceptance holdings of the Reserve banks by $130,000,000. Total reserves of the twelve Federal Reserve banks combined advanced from $2,800,000,000 on March 4, to $3,490,000,000 on April 5, the highest level since the autumn of 1931. On April 7 the discount rate of the Federal Reserve Bank of New York was reduced from 3½ to 3 per cent.[1]

By March 29, about 12,800 banks out of 18,000 in operation before the crisis had been licensed to open on an unrestricted basis, and these banks represented about 90 per cent of the total member-bank deposits of the country.

There is no evidence, either in foreign-exchange rates or in prices, that between the end of February and the end of April there occurred any considerable depreciation in the dollar. In terms of cable transfer rates on gold-standard France, the dollar depreciated 4.4 per cent; in terms of sterling it likewise depreciated 4.4 per cent; wholesale prices rose 1 per cent and the cost of living declined 0.8 per cent, while common stocks showed an average rise of 6.7 per cent. The Federal Reserve Board's index of industrial production rose 4.7 per cent, the Cleveland Trust Company's index of industrial activity

[1] *Federal Reserve Bulletin*, April, 1933, p. 209.

increased 4.9 per cent. The monthly number of commercial failures declined 19 per cent, and their liabilities, 22 per cent.

In other words, business was improving, confidence was returning, and the emergency that had justified temporary drastic measures was passing. Under the circumstances, the wise course for the Administration to have followed was to return to the gold standard at an early date, with full convertibility of paper money into gold and the removal of all restrictions on the exportation and holding of gold, accompanied by a bold assurance from the President that the government was willing if necessary to go to the limit of its resources for the maintenance of the gold standard.

Liberal emergency measures of the general types actually taken to help the debtor classes for a reasonable period, of course, should have been adopted. On this broad question, the following statement, which was made 2 years before by the Macmillan Committee of Great Britain concerning the situation in England, is sound doctrine:[1]

. . . In our opinion the devaluation by any Government of a currency standing at its par value suddenly and without notice . . . is emphatically one of those things which are not expedient. International trade, commerce and finance are based on confidence. One of the foundation stones on which that confidence reposes is the general belief that all countries will seek to maintain so far as lies in their power the value of their national currency as it has been fixed by law, and will

[1] Macmillan Committee, *Report*, pp. 110 and 111.

only give legal recognition to its depreciation when that depreciation has already come about *de facto*. It has frequently been the case—we have numerous examples of recent years—that either through the misfortunes of war, or mistakes of policy, or the collapse of prices, currencies have fallen so far below par that their restoration would involve either great social injustices or national efforts and sacrifices for which no adequate compensation can be expected. . . . *But it would be to adopt an entirely new principle, and one which would undoubtedly be an immense shock to the international financial world, if the Government of the greatest creditor nation were deliberately and by an act of positive policy to announce one morning that it had reduced by law the value of its currency from the par at which it was standing to some lower value . . .* [1] In the atmosphere of crisis and distress which would inevitably surround such an extreme and sensational measure as the devaluation of sterling, we might well find that the state of affairs immediately ensuing on such an event would be worse than that which had preceded it.

Instead of taking action in the late spring of 1933, looking toward an early return to the pre-"bank-holiday" gold standard, the Roosevelt administration resorted to a series of radical measures deliberately depreciating the gold value of the dollar. These measures resulted in the giving up of the gold-coin standard, a permanent debasement of the nation's gold monetary unit, the abrogation of tens of billions of dollars of specific gold contracts, including those of the government itself, the outlawing of the circulation of all United States gold coins and gold certificates, the nationalization of our gold and

[1] The italics are my own.

[127]

silver, and the granting to the President, for more than a decade at least, almost supreme dictatorial power over the nation's currency.

On July 2, 1933, came the President's "bolt of lightning" message to Secretary Hull in London that wrecked the World Economic Conference from which we and the leading countries of Europe had reason to expect much for the cause of international monetary stabilization on a gold basis.

A few months after this, in a radio address on October 22, the President suddenly and without previous public discussion announced the adoption as a United States policy of the Warren gold purchase plan, which was intended to raise commodity prices quickly to the desired level—presumably that of 1926—and thereafter to maintain them at that level, through a system of currency management. The plan, which was not a success, was quietly discontinued early in 1934.[1]

By the end of 1933, practically all hope had gone for any return to the gold-coin standard with the old gold dollar as the legal unit of value.

The New Type of American Gold Standard

The gold reserve law of 1934, which became effective at the end of January, gave to the United States a new legal monetary unit of about the gold value possessed by the paper dollar of that date, and provided the country with a currency system of a

[1] *Cf.* KEMMERER, EDWIN WALTER, *Kemmerer On Money*, Chap. III.

type substantially different from any ever before known throughout the world's monetary history. In this new monetary system there were three outstanding features:

1. The first of these is a statutory stabilization of the dollar, not as previously at a fixed gold value, but, at the discretion of the President, within the fixed range of gold values represented by 50 to 60 cents of the former gold dollar.[1]

This provision of the law was supplemented by an administrative order of the President fixing the gold value of the dollar for the time being at the equivalent of 59.06 cents—a rate that raised the dollar price of an ounce of pure gold from the former statutory price of $20.67 to a new administrative price of $35, representing an increase of 69.3 per cent. The only kind of gold convertibility thenceforward permitted was convertibility, at the option of the government, of the new-type gold certificates,

[1] Even these limits were apparently removed by sections 8, 9, and 10 of the law, which authorized the Secretary of the Treasury to buy gold in unlimited quantities at any price "he may deem most advantageous to the public interest, any provision of law relating to the maintenance of the parity . . . to the contrary notwithstanding" and "to sell gold in any amounts . . . and at such rates . . . as he may deem most advantageous to the public interest . . ."

The authority granted to the President administratively to change the gold content of the dollar at his discretion to anywhere between the equivalent of 50 and 60 per cent of that of the former gold dollar was restricted to 2 years, but was renewed by Congress biennially until 1943. Its nonrenewal in that year was apparently of no consequence, since the above-mentioned sections 8, 9, and 10 of the Act of 1934 were not repealed, and they still seem to give the President the power to change the gold content of the dollar at will without limits.

which could legally be held only by the Federal Reserve banks and by the government. The exportation, holding, and transportation of gold was thenceforth permissible only under the conditions and to the extent that the Secretary of the Treasury, with the approval of the President, should determine by administrative order.

2. The government established a stabilization fund out of its "devaluation profits." When the stabilization law was passed, the national government and the Federal Reserve banks together owned a little over $4 billion of gold coin and gold bullion. Inasmuch as under the devaluation plan the value of the amount of pure gold contained in 59.06 cents worth of old gold coin was to constitute, at least for the time being, the new unit of value, or dollar, this $4 billion of gold coin and bullion was increased in terms of the new dollar by $2,811 million. Since the passage of the stabilization law, additional receipts of gold have raised this profit to about $2,819 million, out of which approximately $2 billion is now held by the government for a stabilization fund, and of this amount a little over $200 million is in use as an active fund.

3. The third noteworthy provision of the stabilization law was the one declaring that legal title to all gold owned by the Federal Reserve authorities should be transferred to the United States government, and should be paid for by the government in the new type of noncirculating "gold certificate."

What is our present monetary standard? The standard created by this new legislation is difficult to define. Legally, it might be classed as a restricted commodity standard, for the law apparently contemplated the possibility of changing the gold value of the dollar according to the ups and downs of the commodity price level. Since the law was enacted, however, there has been no change in the gold content of the dollar, and the law has been administered in such a way as to make the new monetary system a *de facto* gold-bullion standard. So long as the government or its agencies stands ready, in an extensive market like that now provided by the governments and central banks of friendly countries, to buy and sell gold on demand at approximately a fixed gold price—now $35 an ounce—and to permit the gold so sold and bought to be freely exported and imported in unlimited quantities, and to permit the domestic supply of currency to respond to these gold movements, the gold value of the paper dollar will be maintained very close to the value of a fixed quantity of gold in a large, free international market. This is the "constituting quality" of a gold standard.

To the extent, however, that the government interferes with such free exportation and importation of gold or prevents the gold coming into the country from increasing the country's monetary supply by the amount imported or prevents the gold going out from decreasing the monetary supply by the amount exported, or to the extent that the government exercises its legal authority frequently to vary the gold content of the dollar by changing its official price for gold, the gold value of the dollar will tend to depart from the value of a fixed quantity of gold in a large, free, international market, and to that extent we shall depart from the gold standard.

According to the concept of the gold standard thus defined, probably no important country in the world except the United States is now (1944) on the gold standard, or has been for several years. A number of countries, however, now have standards that are close approximations to the gold standard, *e.g.*, Brazil, Colombia, and Venezuela.

SELECTED BIBLIOGRAPHY

CRAWFORD, ARTHUR WHIPPLE: *Monetary Management under the New Deal*, American Council on Public Affairs, Washington, D.C., 1940.

Cunliffe Committee: Committee on Currency and Foreign Exchanges, *Report*, His Majesty's Stationery Office, London, 1918.

Director of the Mint: *Monetary Systems of the Principal Countries of the World*, Government Printing Office, Washington, D.C., 1917.

GREGORY, T. E.: *The Gold Standard and Its Future*, Methuen & Co., Ltd., London, 1932.

———: Britain and the Gold Standard, *Foreign Affairs*, January, 1933.

HARRIS, S. E.: *Monetary Problems of the British Empire*, The Macmillan Company, New York, 1931.

HAWTREY, R. G.: The Gold Standard, *Economic Journal*, December, 1919.

Hoover, Herbert: *Addresses upon the American Road*, 1933–1938, Charles Scribner's Sons, New York, 1938.

Kemmerer, Edwin Walter: Gold and the Gold Standard, *Proceedings of the American Philosophical Society*, vol. LXXI, 1932.

————: *Kemmerer on Money*, 2d ed., John C. Winston Company, Philadelphia, 1934.

————: *The A B C of Inflation*, McGraw-Hill Book Company, Inc., New York, 1942.

————: *Inflation and Revolution*, Princeton University Press, Princeton, N.J., 1940.

Keynes, Lord John Maynard: *A Treatise on Money*, 2 vols., Harcourt, Brace and Company, New York, 1930.

Layton, W. T.: British Opinion of the Gold Standard, *Quarterly Journal of Economics*, February, 1925.

Lehfeldt, R. A.: *A Restoration of the World's Currencies*, P. S. King & Son, Ltd., London, 1923.

Macmillan Committee: Committee on Finance and Industry, *Report* and *Minutes of Evidence*, 3 vols., His Majesty's Stationery Office, London, 1931.

Myers, William Starr, and Walter H. Newton: *The Hoover Administration*, Charles Scribner's Sons, New York, 1936.

Rist, Charles: *La Déflation en pratique*, Marcel Giard, Paris, 1924.

Roosevelt, Franklin D.: *The Public Papers and Addresses*, 9 vols., Random House, Inc., New York, 1940.

Wilbur, Ray Lyman, and Arthur Mastick Hyde: *The Hoover Policies*, Charles Scribner's Sons, New York, 1937.

Young, John Parke: *European Currency and Finance*, Commission of Gold and Silver Inquiry, vols. I and II. United States Senate. Government Printer, Washington, D.C., 1925.

————: Inter-war Currency Lessons, No. 9: The Monetary Standards Inquiry, New York, 1944.

CHAPTER V

Characteristics of the Gold Standard

Gold presents . . . a combination of useful and striking properties quite without parallel among known substances.—
W. STANLEY JEVONS, 1875.

This chapter will attempt to explain briefly the outstanding characteristics of the genus *gold standard* and the following chapter will describe its three principal species.

WHAT CONSTITUTES A GOLD STANDARD

Definition and Explanation

From the preceding historical discussion the reader has seen the nature of the generic gold standard. This standard may be briefly defined as a monetary system where the unit of value, in terms of which prices, wages, and debts are customarily expressed and paid, consists of the value of a fixed quantity of gold in a large international market which is substantially free.[1]

---

[1] Obviously, for the gold standard to function, the international market must be more than a very narrow one, and obviously, also, it is unrealistic to expect a market that is 100 per cent free.

This definition calls for some explanation. It contains no mention of gold coin or of free coinage of gold. Both of these may be of great convenience and may facilitate the efficient operation of a gold standard, but neither is necessary to the existence of a gold standard. The gold-bullion standard and the gold-exchange standard, which are described in the next chapter, do not ordinarily make any provision for the minting and circulation of gold coins, but both of these standards are clearly forms of the gold standard.

The definition makes no mention of legal tender, a useful quality for standard money to possess but not a necessary one. Legal tender is a purely legal concept of late historical development, usually relating only to debt-paying rights, and a gold standard can exist and perform all of its necessary functions without any legal-tender laws whatsoever. On the other hand, full legal-tender money has at times been driven out of circulation through the force of Gresham's law[1] or of custom by non-legal-tender money.

[1] The monetary principle known as *Gresham's law*, although Sir Thomas Gresham had little to do with its discovery, is merely an application to money of the economic law of demand and supply. This is the law that says an economic good tends to go to the best market. The law superficially appears to operate somewhat differently for money than for other economic goods, because money is unique in the fact that one of its principal functions is that of passing from hand to hand as a commonly accepted medium of exchange. A precise formulation of Gresham's law within a few words is impossible. With minor qualifications, however, the law may be briefly stated as follows: When two or more kinds of money are in circulation in the same market, all enjoying essentially the same privileges under the law, custom, and public opinion, the poorest money will drive the better money or moneys out of circulation;

There is no mention in the definition of redeemability in gold (or its equivalent) of paper money and of fiduciary coins, which is a privilege in most successful gold-standard systems. This privilege is highly desirable, but it is not necessary, provided that sufficient other effective means are used for maintaining the parity of the different kinds of money with the gold unit, such as limiting their supply and receiving them without limit in payment of taxes and other public dues.

All the above-mentioned qualities are useful devices for maintaining the gold standard, but not one of them is absolutely necessary. Furthermore, a currency system might conceivably have any or even all of them and still not be a true gold standard.

A good illustration of the principle here discussed is found in the experience of the Union of South Africa in 1919 and 1920.[1] At that time gold sovereigns, which were unlimited legal tender in the Union,

provided that the total supply of all kinds of money in circulation is sufficiently large to make *money* so cheap that the better money is worth more outside of active circulation for hoards, merchandise, or export than in such circulation; and provided further, that a dual or other multiple currency system does not develop, under which there are different commodity prices for payments made in the different currencies.

The reader interested in an historical exemplification of the need for the many qualifications included in the above formulation of Gresham's law will find it in the experiences of the Philippine Islands prior to and shortly following the American occupation in 1898, and during the years 1903 to 1907. See Kemmerer, Edwin Walter, *Modern Currency Reforms*, pp. 245–292 and 324–346.

[1] RICHARDS, C. S., *Currency in South Africa before Union*, reprinted in Kemmerer-Vissering, *Report on the Resumption of Gold Payments by the Union of South Africa*, p. 537.

and which enjoyed the free-coinage privilege in England—there was no mint in the Union of South Africa—circulated freely in the Union, and the bank notes there were redeemable at their respective banks of issue in gold sovereigns on demand at parity. However, the exportation of gold bullion from the Union was rigidly controlled by the Government. South African gold coins could not be legally exported to what would otherwise have been their best market, but were extensively smuggled out of the country and sold for more than the foreign-currency equivalent of a South African pound. A sovereign in South Africa, and likewise the gold bullion content of a sovereign, were worth there less than in the outside free-gold markets of the world. In order to get the sovereigns with which to redeem their notes on demand, as required by law, the South African banks of issue were compelled to buy raw gold in London at a premium, to get it coined in London in the usual way at the British mint, and then to bring it to South Africa. At times they had to pay as much as 26 or 28 shillings of South African bank notes to obtain a sovereign in England. The sovereign was then paid out in South Africa by the bank of issue in redemption at par of a 20-shilling bank note.

Monetary history offers many instances of gold coins dammed up in a country and circulating there at a discount from their bullion value in outside free markets.[1]

[1] See KEMMERER, EDWIN WALTER, Mexico's Monetary Experience in 1917,

On the other hand, a governmental prohibition on the importation of gold in a supposedly gold-standard country, by restricting the supply within the country, might force up the value of gold bullion and gold coin within the country above their values in the free international markets and thereby give them an artificial scarcity or monopoly value.

Whenever the gold value of the monetary unit of a country is divorced from the market value of gold in the free markets of the world, the country cannot be said to be on a true gold standard.

Regardless, therefore, of which of the many common means may be adopted by a nation to maintain the value of its money, such as convertibility, legal tender, and free coinage, the supreme test of the existence of the gold standard is the answer to the question whether or not the money of the country is actually kept at a parity with the value of the gold monetary unit comprising it, in the outside free international gold market, assuming, of course, that such a market of reasonable size actually exists. It is not a question of the means adopted to obtain a particular result, but rather, one of the result itself. The gold standard exists then in any country whenever the value of a fixed quantity of gold in a large and substantially free international market is actually maintained as the standard unit of value.

American Economic Review, Supplement, March, 1918, pp. 261–262; also, the experiences of the Scandinavian countries and of Spain, 1916–1919, in the *Federal Reserve Bulletin*, 1919, pp. 1039–1042, and 1920, pp. 35–46.

The Monetary Unit—a Fixed Weight, Not a Fixed Value

Under a gold standard (as well as under any other metallic-money standard), it is the weight of the metallic content of the monetary unit that is fixed and not the value, which is an expression of purchasing power. In this respect the unit of value differs from all other units of measurement. For example, the pound as a unit of weight is a fixed weight, the yard as a unit of length is a fixed length, and the gallon as a unit of volume is a fixed volume.[1] The gold dollar, however, which is our American unit of value, is whatever value is attached at a particular moment to a fixed weight of pure gold, now, one thirty-fifth of an ounce Troy. This value, like the value of anything else, is a continually changing thing—a fact that gives rise to our most difficult monetary problems.

GOLD AS A MONEY METAL

From the monetary standpoint, gold possesses certain well-known physical qualities, which have never been better described than by W. Stanley Jevons in his classic little book, *Money and the Mechanism of Exchange*, from which much of the material in this paragraph is taken. Largely by

[1] These units of measurement in advanced countries are determined meticulously by law. For example, the British Imperial standard yard is defined by law as the distance at 62°F. between two fine lines engraved on gold studs, sunk in a bronze bar, which is in the possession of the government.

[139]

reason of its beauty and its scarcity, gold has been a commodity of universal demand for countless generations, being prized highly by the most primitive peoples as well as by the most advanced. Possessing a large value in a small bulk, it is easily transported. Pure gold is homogeneous, *i.e.*, uniform throughout the mass, so that equal weights will always have exactly the same value. Like other metals, but unlike skins, precious stones, and most other commodities, gold has the quality of divisibility without loss. A nugget of gold can be cut into pieces without loss and the pieces in turn may be readily restored to the original form, likewise without loss. Gold is very durable, being

remarkable for its freedom from corrosion or solution [and] being quite unaffected and untarnished after exposure of any length of time to dry, or moist, or impure air, and being also insoluble in all the simple acids. . . . In almost all respects gold is perfectly suited for coining. When quite pure, indeed, it is almost as soft as tin, but when alloyed with one tenth or one twelfth part of copper, becomes sufficiently hard to resist wear and tear, and to give a good metallic ring; yet it remains perfectly malleable and takes a fine impression.[1]

Because of its high value it is carefully guarded by its owners. This fact and the great durability of gold largely explain its high degree of stability in value. There is gold in the world today that men extracted from nature thousands of years before Christ. Our present supply is the "accumulation of

[1] JEVONS, W. STANLEY, *Money and the Mechanism of Exchange*, pp. 46–47.

the ages," and most of it can readily be made marketable, since it is largely in relatively unspecialized forms, such as coins and bars. The world's annual production of gold, which, for a number of years prior to the Second World War, was approximately equivalent to only about 4 per cent of the world's known stock of monetary gold, acts very slowly in affecting the value of such a large marketable supply.

The Demand for Gold, Highly Elastic

Gold is a commodity of highly elastic demand; in fact, it probably has the most elastic demand of all commodities on the market in a gold-standard country. All three of the principal kinds of demand for gold are highly elastic; They are (1) the monetary demand, (2) the demand for the purpose of ornamentation, including jewelry and utensils, and (3) the hoarding demand.

The Monetary Demand. The demand for gold for monetary uses is obviously highly elastic when the principal countries of the world are on a gold standard and when these countries are offering to buy at fixed prices in unlimited amounts all the gold offered to them for monetary purposes.

The Demand for Ornamentation. The demand for gold to use in ornamentation is likewise highly elastic. Primitive man's first form of clothing was probably some form of paint or mud on his skin— in other words, ornament. Clothing for protection came later. The desire for ornamentation from that

[141]

day to this has been universal and practically unlimited. Gold is the most widely treasured material
for articles of beauty. Most people in the world
would like to have more gold ornaments than they
do possess and would buy more if such articles were
to become cheaper. Reductions in the value of gold
ornaments and utensils as compared with other
goods, therefore, stimulate an increased demand, and
this demand acts as a buffer to gold depreciation.

The Hoarding Demand. The demand for gold
for the purpose of hoarding is, again, highly elastic.
The practice of hoarding gold, common to all countries of the world, is resorted to increasingly in
times of unsettlement and fear. It is especially
prevalent in India and China. Gold, to the Oriental
peoples who hoard it, is a symbol of wealth in general.
A given quantity of gold jewelry is not only a commodity that gives direct enjoyment to the Hindu
farmer, but it is also a blank check, which he can
fill out at any time with the name of any commodity
he may want at its market price, a check that can be
cashed on demand. His gold trinkets and jewelry
serve as his savings-bank deposit and his insurance
policy against famine and other misfortune. The
capacity of India and China to absorb gold and
silver in hoards is well known. For many generations
India was known as the "sink" of the precious
metals. From 1931, however, when India went off
the gold standard and the price of gold in terms of
Indian rupees, instead of continuing stable, ad-

vanced greatly, through 1940, India's hoarded gold was poured onto the world's markets at rates even greater than those at which it was previously accumulated.[1]

This high degree of elasticity of demand is an important factor in maintaining the high stability of value that gold possesses.

Characteristics of Gold in Its Relation to the Gold Standard

Gold in its relation to the gold standard has three important characteristics.[2] Although they are not entirely distinct, they are best considered separately. These characteristics are (1) a fixed price, (2) an unlimited market, and (3) the fact that normally the production of gold from year to year is controlled chiefly by changing costs in its production and not by changing prices of the product itself.

A Fixed Price. When a government adopts a gold standard, it fixes the gold content of the monetary unit. Prior to 1933, for example, the unit of value in the United States was defined as the dollar consisting of 25.8 grains of gold 0.900[3] fine, which means 90 per cent was pure gold and 10 per cent was copper alloy, making the fine-gold content of the dollar 23.22 grains. Since there are 480 grains in a troy

[1] See *Federal Reserve Bulletin*, 1935, p. 822, and 1943, p. 1201.

[2] These three characteristics would apply also to silver under a silver standard and to both gold and silver under a system of successful bimetallism.

[3] Act of March 14, 1900, Section 1.

ounce, an ounce of gold was equivalent to as many dollars as $\frac{480}{23.22}$ or $20.67, and could always be coined into that amount of gold coin. To say that the dollar was 23.22 grains of pure gold and to say that the mint price of gold was $20.67 were identical propositions. It was like saying that a foot is 12 inches and that an inch is one-twelfth of a foot.[1] Gold coin, on the other hand, at any time could be melted down and reconverted into gold bars. Except for a brief period at the time of the First World War, there were from 1879 to 1933 no restrictions or tariff charges on the importation and exportation of gold.

An Unlimited Market. Not only was the price of gold always the same at the mint and assay offices, but these concerns were under obligation to buy all gold presented to them in proper form, no matter whether it was produced within the United States or abroad or whether it was new gold or gold obtained from the melting down of foreign coins or from jewelry, ornaments, or other sources.[2]

The Production of Gold, Correlated Inversely with the Prices of Other Commodities. The third characteristic of gold in its relation to the gold standard is the

---

[1] Our mint and assay offices (after January 14, 1873) made no charges to anyone for the process of coining gold brought to them, but did charge depositors of gold bullion small fees to cover such costs as those for melting, refining, and alloy.

[2] A like free-coinage privilege would apply to silver in a silver-standard country and to both gold and silver in a bimetallic country.

peculiar relationship of its market price to the volume of its current production.

In the case of other commodities, production normally increases as their market prices advance and production decreases as their market prices fall. This, however, is not true for gold in a gold-standard country. Here, as has been previously pointed out, the price of gold does not change. For example, between 1879 and 1916, inclusive, in the United States, no matter how much gold was being produced in the world's markets or how little, the price of pure gold at the mint was always $20.67 an ounce; and, although during these 38 years the world's annual production of gold increased fourfold and the value or purchasing power of an ounce of gold varied continually and at some times substantially, the price of gold never changed. The reason was that our gold-standard system itself fixed the price of gold, while it did not and could not fix the value of gold.

Although gold producers always received the same price for their gold at the mint and assay offices, the costs of producing this gold were continually changing, as the value or the purchasing power of the gold changed. An increase in the production of gold relative to the demand tends to increase the supply of monetary gold and of the other money and deposit-currency circulation that is based upon it, and thereby, through increasing commodity prices, tends to make gold less valuable. The commodities whose prices are thus increased include, among others, all those that are elements in the cost of mining gold itself, such as explosives and other chemicals, mining machinery, and labor; also, taxes. It is these rising costs pressing against a fixed gold price that tend to reduce gold production by cutting into the mine owners' profits when the value of gold is declining.

On the other hand, when the value of gold is increasing, *i.e.*, when commodity prices are falling, the prices of the things that comprise mining costs tend to fall with the prices of other commodities. This reduces the cost of mining and, since the mine owner continues to sell all of his gold at the same mint price as before, his profits are increased and gold production is stimulated. *Therefore, the production of gold tends to increase when the value of gold rises and to decrease when that value falls.*

It should be noted, parenthetically, that gold is produced under widely varying conditions in different parts of the world, that considerable gold is produced as a by-product of other metals, and that much is still obtained in backward places by primitive methods of panning; while large amounts of labor are continually being spent in more or less futile efforts to find pay dirt. All this means that at any one time it is difficult to ascertain just what is the cost of producing gold. The significant cost, the economist would say, is the marginal cost in the gold mines of substantial gold-producing areas like those of the Transvaal and Russia. This marginal cost, however, is not easily located.

Monetary Gold versus Gold in the Arts

When the value of gold falls and the commodity price level rises, the price of the gold used in manufacturing jewelry, utensils, etc., does not rise, although the costs of other materials and of labor involved in their manufacture and marketing will advance. This means that the prices of articles made largely of gold do not advance in times of rising price levels as much as do wages and the prices of most other commodities. Gold jewelry and other gold articles, therefore, at such times appear cheap as compared with most other goods, and this situation stimulates demand for them, thereby increasing the flow of newly mined gold into the arts and diverting old gold into the arts from monetary uses. The hoarding of gold ornaments, trinkets, and bullion is also stimulated, particularly in countries like India and China, where there is usually an enormous demand for such commodities. All this tends to hold back the upward movement of general prices and the reduction in gold-mining profits that results from them.

When, on the other hand, commodity prices are falling and the value of gold is rising, we have the opposite situation. Then the prices of jewelry, ornaments, and other gold manufactures do not fall as much as the prices of most other things and as wages, because the price of gold itself does not fall. This makes gold products appear dear to the consumer and, therefore, lessens the demand for them. It drives into the money uses gold that would otherwise have gone into the arts, and causes the melting down of gold jewelry and ornaments in India and China and the flow of the gold bullion obtained therefrom into the money uses. Gold in the money uses is thereby made more plentiful, and this fact tends to check the declining commodity prices and the rising gold-mining profits.

SELECTED BIBLIOGRAPHY

ARNDT, E. H. D.: *Banking and Currency Developments in South Africa* (1652–1927), Juta & Co., Ltd., Cape Town, 1928.

DeKock, M. H.: *The Economic Development of South Africa,* P. S. King & Son, Ltd., London, 1936.

———: *Economic History of South Africa,* Juta & Co., Ltd., Cape Town, 1924.

Federal Reserve Bulletins, 1919, 1920, 1935, and 1943.

FETTER, FRANK WHITSON: Gresham's Law and the Chilean Peso, *Journal of Political Economy,* vol. 41 (1933).

Gold Policy and Foreign Commerce of the Scandinavian Countries, 1914–1919, *Federal Reserve Bulletin,* 1920.

GRAHAM, FRANK D., and CHARLES R. WHITTLESEY: *Golden Avalanche,* Princeton University Press, Princeton, N.J., 1939.

GREGORY, T. E.: *The Gold Standard and Its Future,* E. P. Dutton & Company, Inc., New York, 1931.

JEVONS, W. STANLEY: *Money and the Mechanism of Exchange,* D. Appleton-Century Company, Inc., New York, 1875.

KEMMERER, EDWIN WALTER: Mexico's Monetary Experience in 1917, *American Economic Review,* Supplement, March, 1918.

———: *Modern Currency Reforms*, The Macmillan Company, New York, 1916.

———: Gold and the Gold Standard, *Proceedings of the American Philosophical Society*, vol. LXXI (1932).

———, and GERARD VISSERING: *Report on the Resumption of Gold Payments by the Union of South Africa*, Government Printing and Stationery Office, Pretoria, 1925.

KEYNES, LORD JOHN MAYNARD: *A Treatise on Money*, vol. II, The Applied Theory of Money, Harcourt, Brace and Company, New York, 1930.

———: *A Tract on Monetary Reform*, Macmillan & Company, Ltd., London, 1923.

League of Nations: *Interim Report of the Gold Delegation of the Financial Committee*, Geneva, 1930.

———: *Second Interim Report*, 1931.

———: *Report of the Gold Delegation of the Financial Committee*, Geneva, 1932.

———: *Selected Documents Submitted to the Gold Delegation of the Financial Committee*, Geneva, 1930.

———: *Selected Documents on the Distribution of Gold Submitted to the Gold Delegation of the Financial Commitee*, Geneva, 1931.

Macmillan Committee: Committee on Finance and Industry, *Report* and *Minutes of Evidence*, 3 vols., His Majesty's Stationery Office, London, 1931.

NORMAN WAIT HARRIS MEMORIAL FOUNDATION: *Gold and Monetary Stabilization*, *Report of Round Tables*, 1932, mimeographed, The University of Chicago, Chicago, 1932.

RICHARDS, C. S.: *Currency in South Africa before Union*, reprinted in the Kemmerer-Vissering *Report on the Resumption of Gold Payments by the Union of South Africa*, Government Printing and Stationery Office, Pretoria, 1925.

ROGERS, JAMES HARVEY: *America Weighs Her Gold*, Yale University Press, New Haven, 1931.

Royal Institute of International Affairs: *The International Gold Problem*, Oxford University Press, London, 1931.

Spain's Foreign Commerce and Finance, 1914–1919, *Federal Reserve Bulletin*, 1919.

Touzet, André: *Emplois industriels des métaux precieux*, V. Girard et E. Brière, Paris, 1911.

Union of South Africa: *Report of the Select Committee on the Gold Standard*, Cape Times, Ltd., Cape Town, 1932.

————: *Report of the Select Committee on Embargo on Export of Specie*, Cape Times, Ltd., Cape Town, 1920.

CHAPTER VI

Varieties of the Gold Standard

It takes all sorts to make a world.—ENGLISH PROVERB, 1620.

Historically speaking, as we have seen, and taking in our survey the whole world, there have been many ways in which gold has functioned as standard money, both outside a formally organized gold-standard system and as part of such a system. All important gold-standard systems, however, may be conveniently grouped into three species, *viz.*, the gold-coin standard, the gold-exchange standard, and the gold-bullion standard, while each of these species appears in many varieties, both alone and in combination with the other two. The gold-exchange standard and the gold-bullion standard, in their modern forms, are institutions of the late nineteenth and early twentieth centuries, although their roots reach deep into the past.

THE GOLD-COIN STANDARD

By far the most important form of the gold standard has been the gold-coin standard. This is the form that is chiefly contemplated in the last four chapters of this book. Since the varietal characteristics of the gold-coin standard have already been considered, a mere summary of them here will be sufficient. They may, then, be summed up as follows: The parity of all forms of money and of deposit currency is maintained with the value of a gold monetary unit, which is coined (singly or in multiples), under a system of free coinage, without appreciable charge for the coinage process. Gold coins are permitted to circulate freely throughout the country, may be freely exported and imported, may be melted, are unlimited legal tender, and are acceptable without limit in payment of all taxes and other government dues. They constitute all, or a large part of, the country's central monetary reserve, which functions as a regulator fund to maintain the parity of the nation's money by adjusting the supply of money and of deposit currency to the ever-changing demands of trade.

The manner in which the gold-coin standard functions will be somewhat further clarified by the following explanation of the gold-exchange standard, because all three varieties of the gold standard (gold-coin, gold-exchange, and gold-bullion) function on the same fundamental principles.

The Gold-exchange Standard

Although crude plans suggestive of the modern gold-exchange standard were proposed from time to time during the eighteenth and the early nineteenth century,[1] and some of them were used, the first fully

---

[1] See, for example, the currency plan for British colonies and dependencies outlined in a Treasury Minute of February 11, 1825, which is described by E. H. D. Arndt, in his *Banking and Currency Development in South Africa*, p. 45.

worked-out gold-exchange standard plan was that of A. M. Lindsay of the Bank of Bengal, which he recommended for India, first in 1876 and repeatedly thereafter. He presented the Lindsay plan in a complete form in his testimony before the Indian Currency Committee of 1898.[1] In his elaboration and defense of his plan, Mr. Lindsay did a masterly job and probably contributed more than anyone else toward making the idea of the gold-exchange standard current coin. The Indian government rejected the plan at the time, but adopted it in its essentials a few years later.[2]

Principles of the Gold-exchange Standard as Exemplified in the Philippines, 1905–1910

Several countries, including Java, India, and Austria-Hungary, adopted the gold-exchange standard before the end of the nineteenth century, and between 1920 and 1930 literally scores of countries adopted the principle of the gold-exchange standard to a greater or less extent. Nonetheless, the nearest approach to the simon-pure gold-exchange standard that the world has yet seen was the currency system of the Philippine Islands as it was administered from 1905 to about 1910 under the Philippine Gold Standard Act of 1903. A description of the essentials of

[1] For references to Lindsay's early writings on the subject and a summary of his plan, see Edwin Walter Kemmerer's *Modern Currency Reforms*, pp. 79–92. For Lindsay's elaboration and defense of the plan, see Fowler Committee, *Report*, Evidence, Questions, 3275–4303.

[2] KEMMERER, *op. cit.*, pp. 100–108.

[153]

this system will be the best way to make clear the fundamentals of the gold-exchange standard.[1]

At the beginning of this period the currency of the Philippine Islands consisted chiefly of fiduciary silver coins and silver certificates, fractional coins, and for a brief time considerable United States paper money.

The Philippine Coinage Act passed by the United States Congress, March 2, 1903, had declared that the unit of value of the Philippine Islands should be a theoretical gold peso (not coined), consisting of 12.9 grains of gold, 0.900 fine, and therefore exactly equivalent to 50 cents of United States gold coin of that time. The law required that the silver peso and all the fractional coins of the Islands should be kept at parity with this gold peso.

For maintaining the parity, the Philippine Gold Standard Act of October 10, 1903, enacted by the Philippine Government under the authority of the above-mentioned law, created a special reserve fund known as the *gold-standard fund*. This fund was composed of the proceeds of a loan floated in the United States, of all seigniorage profits realized in the coinage of the new money, and of certain other profits incidental to the administration of the currency. It was a trust fund, kept separate from all other government funds, and was to be used exclusively for the maintenance of the gold parity of

---

[1] The following description is a revision and abridgement of the author's article on the Gold-exchange Standard in *Economic Essays in Honour of Gustav Cassel*, pp. 311–326.

the Philippine currency. The law provided that part of the fund should be kept in Manila and part in the United States.

For the maintenance of the parity the principal form of redemption[1] was in gold drafts on New York. The Philippine treasurer was directed to sell, on demand for Philippine currency, drafts in sums of not less than $5,000 (the equivalent of the conventional gold bar of commerce) on that part of the gold-standard fund kept on deposit in American banks,[2] charging for the same a premium of ¾ of 1 per cent for demand drafts and of 1⅛ per cent for telegraphic transfers. It was likewise provided in the law that banks in the United States that acted as depositories of the gold-standard fund should sell drafts in sums of not less than 10,000 pesos on that part of the gold-standard fund held in the treasury vaults in Manila, payable in Philippine currency, charging for them the same premium rates.

All Philippine currency brought to the Philippine Treasury for the purchase of exchange on the United States, pursuant to the above provisions of law, was required immediately to be withdrawn from circulation *and physically kept in the treasury vaults.* The money so withdrawn from circulation, with certain qualifications, could not be paid out again, except in response to drafts drawn by a gold-standard fund depository

---

[1] For a more detailed account of this system see Kemmerer, *Modern Currency Reforms*, pp. 317–323.

[2] The fund in the United States was kept largely in one or two New York City banks.

bank in the United States, on the fund in Manila, or for the purchase of silver to provide a needed increase in coinage.

The object of the sale of drafts was to provide a means for maintaining the gold parity. Every important function of a gold currency, except that of shipment to and from other countries in making international payments, it was claimed, could be performed as well by the Philippine silver and paper currency as by gold coin. This Philippine silver and paper currency, it was said, was better adapted than gold coin would have been to the needs of Philippine trade and to the tastes of the great majority of the Filipino people. Some provision, however, had to be made for the performance of that essential function of money, the function of making international payments, which could not be performed by Philippine fiduciary money. This function of money, or of bullion promptly exchangeable for money on demand, is important not only because it provides a means by which foreign payments are made, but still more so because through it the currency supply is kept adjusted to the currency demand, and the parity is maintained by a reduction of the supply of money in circulation in times of its relative redundancy and by an increase of the supply in times of its relative scarcity.

When, in the trade among gold-standard countries, the balance of payments becomes strongly unfavorable in one of them, exchange rates rise to the gold-export point, registering a relative redundancy of the home currency, gold is exported, and the currency supply is contracted. Likewise, it is true that, when the balance of payments becomes strongly favorable in one of the countries, exchange rates there fall to the gold-import point, registering a relative scarcity of the home currency, gold is imported, and the currency supply is expanded. Gold will ordinarily be shipped only when the exchange drawn against the shipment will be sufficient to yield some profit after the payment of all the expenses of shipping, including packing, cartage, freight, insurance, interest, and loss from abrasion.

When exchange rates in Manila on New York rose to the gold-export point, gold bars (or gold coins) were not exported, as they would have been under similar circumstances in a gold-coin standard country like the United States, but the Philippine government gave the would-be gold exporter, in exchange for his Philippine currency in Manila, a draft (in multiples of $5,000) entitling him to the gold credit in New York, and charged him as a premium for the draft simply the amount that the actual exportation of the equivalent in gold bars from Manila to New York would have cost him, had he exported the gold himself. The Philippine pesos paid to the government for the draft (exclusive of the premium) were equivalent at parity to the amount of gold he would have shipped. They (including the premium charged) were withdrawn from circulation by the Philippine government and stored in the vaults of the gold-standard fund—a procedure that reduced the circulation of Philippine currency as effectively as the actual exportation of an equivalent amount of Philippine gold coins would have done.

On the other hand, when exchange rates in Manila on New York fell to Manila's gold-import point (which would mean that in New York rates on Manila had risen to New York's gold-export point), a depository of the Philippine gold-standard fund in New York gave the would-be gold exporter in New York, in exchange for his gold (or its equivalent in United States currency), a draft entitling him to the equivalent in Philippine pesos laid down in Manila, and charged him (for the credit of the Philippine gold-standard fund in New York) a premium sufficient to cover the expenses that he would have incurred under the gold-coin standard, had he actually shipped the equivalent in gold bars (or gold coin) from New York to Manila. When the drafts on the gold-standard fund were presented in Manila for payment, they were paid in pesos that were *physically withdrawn from the vaults* of the gold-standard fund, and this payment increased the Philippine currency circulation as truly as would the importation into the islands of an equivalent amount of Philippine gold coins.

The system was just as automatic in its adjustment of the money supply to the needs of trade in the Philippines as a gold-coin standard would have been, although there was no gold coin in circulation and no *gold* reserve was there required. Normally the government had nothing to do with the commercial exchanges, except at the gold-shipping points. These points represented the limits of fluctuation in the gold-exchange value of the peso, which the government imposed. When exchange rates rose to the gold-export point, the government virtually said, "So far they may rise and no farther. A further advance would signify a depreciation of our peso below its legal gold par if we were on a gold-coin standard, and it will be so interpreted under the gold-exchange standard; therefore, we will sell on demand gold drafts on New York in unlimited quantities at these gold-export point rates, and will relieve the currency redundancy by withdrawing from circulation the pesos paid to us for these drafts."

On the other hand, when exchange rates in Manila fell to the gold-import point, the government virtually said, "So far they may fall and no farther; a further decline would signify an appreciation of our peso above its legal gold parity if we were on a gold-coin standard, and it will be so interpreted under the gold-exchange standard; therefore, we will sell on demand pesos laid down in Manila in unlimited quantities at these gold-import point rates, to be paid for by gold or its equivalent in New York. This will relieve the currency scarcity in the islands by pouring pesos into circulation from the gold-standard fund." Commercial exchange rates, therefore, could not rise or fall appreciably beyond these respective limits, and between them the government normally had nothing to do with exchange. That was the field of the banks.

Advantages of the Gold-exchange Standard to the Philippines

The advantages to the Philippines of the gold-exchange standard over a strict gold-coin standard were two-fold. (1) The gold-exchange standard enabled the country to have a circulating medium of the kind best adapted to its needs. Gold coin was not well fitted to the needs of the Philippines, the great bulk of whose transactions were small. Silver and paper were much better. (2) There was the advantage of economy, and this was a matter of great importance to a country like the Philippines, which wanted to be on a gold basis but could not afford the luxury of a gold-coin or even of a gold-bullion standard. Although possibly a larger gold reserve was needed under the gold-exchange standard than would have been needed under a gold-coin standard, the net expense was not proportionately so large. This was true for several reasons: (*a*) The money of circulation was all fiduciary money and therefore much less expensive than it would have been if a large part of it were full-weight gold coins. No gold coins and no gold bars were hoarded, and no gold reserve was maintained in the country to meet the possible demands of would-be hoarders. Conversion of local money into gold was normally made only through foreign drafts, of which the minimum amount sold was the equivalent of a gold bar of $5,000. (*b*) Under the Philippine gold-exchange standard the country's monetary gold was more effective than under a gold-coin standard, as it was all in one reservoir (*e.g.*, the gold-standard fund), where every dollar could be immediately used in time of need; whereas, gold coin in circulation and gold bars in private hands are difficult to mobilize in emergencies. The very emergency that creates the demand for the gold often causes the public to cling to it more tightly. (*c*) The premiums realized by the government on exchange yielded the reserve fund a good profit. (*d*) The part of the gold-standard fund deposited abroad earned interest.

Except under unusual circumstances, the Philippine gold-standard fund continually increased in amount. This was true because (aside from the slight expenses connected with the currency administration that were chargeable to the fund) money was never paid out of the fund at one office (Manila or New York) except in return for a larger sum paid into the fund in the other office. Whenever the fund was temporarily reduced for the purchase of silver (or nickel or copper) to meet the need of new coinage, it was later increased by the new coins to the amount withdrawn, and, in addition, by the net seigniorage profits on the new coinage.

The only times when the fund could be materially depleted in amount (aside from the remotely possible losses by theft or by failure of a depository bank) were times of extreme business depression, when, because of a great decline in business, the currency needs of the country might fall off decidedly and remain below normal for a considerable period of time. Under such contingencies, the silver peso reserve in Manila might be unduly increased by the continually heavy purchases in Manila of drafts on New York, and the gold part of the fund in New York might be correspondingly depleted by the payment of these drafts.

If the depression were so severe that the movement was not checked by the usual forces before the danger point was reached, the gold fund in New York could be replenished through the forward sale in New York by cable from Manila of a few million ounces of silver, to be obtained by the government through the breaking up of the excess pesos held in the peso part of the fund in Manila. The gold proceeds of this sale of silver bullion would then be deposited to the credit of the fund in New York. Here the fund would suffer a loss of the difference between the nominal, or money, value of the pesos broken up and sold as silver and the price obtained for the silver bullion, to which would be added the expenses of the transaction. This would be the opposite of a seigniorage profit—a sort of negative seigniorage. Such a measure would be adopted only as a last resort, however, and the need for taking this step would be evidence that for the existing trade needs too many pesos had been coined. The Philippines never had such an experience.

Under ordinary circumstances the depletion of the gold fund in New York would be checked before it had gone far by processes analogous to those that normally prevent an undue exportation of gold from a gold-coin standard country.[1] They are, notably, (1) a tightening of the money market in Manila through the withdrawal from active circulation and from bank reserves of the large quantities of pesos physically deposited in the gold-standard fund vaults of Manila, (2) the stimulus given to merchandise exports by the prevailing high exchange rates, and (3) the retardation of merchandise imports caused by the same high rates.

The Gold-exchange Standard and the First World War

Prior to the First World War there was a considerable development of the gold-exchange standard along the lines of the standards of the Philippines and India. This was particularly true in colonies and other dependencies and in small countries. In 1914, Keynes wrote,[2] "It may fairly be said . . . that in the last ten years the Gold-exchange Standard has become the prevailing monetary system of Asia."

When in 1914 the war came, metallic-money standards throughout the world broke down, and for

---

[1] For a further discussion of this subject, see Kemmerer, *Money*, pp. 136–140.

[2] KEYNES, LORD JOHN MAYNARD, *Indian Currency and Finance*, p. 36.

years people nearly everywhere found themselves on widely fluctuating paper-money standards. After peace was restored and the world again turned longingly to the gold standard as the only monetary standard in which it had confidence, the gold-exchange standard came forward with a strong appeal. It was the least expensive form of the gold standard known, and this was an important consideration in a war-bankrupt world. It was also the form that was most economical in the use of gold. This likewise was important, because gold production had greatly declined from 1915 to 1922, and there was much public concern about the adequacy of the world's future supply of gold to meet the requirements of a world-wide return to the yellow metal.

The Genoa International Conference
and the Gold-exchange Standard

The Genoa International Conference in 1922 took a strong stand in favor of the gold-exchange standard.[1] Its principal recommendations relating to this subject are these:[2]

Measures of currency reform will be facilitated if the practice of continuous cooperation among central banks of issue . . . in the several countries can be developed. . . . In countries where there is no central bank of issue one should be established. . . . It is desirable that all European currencies should be based upon a common standard. . . . Gold is the

---

[1] Genoa Conference, *Papers Relating to International Economic Conference, Genoa*, April–May, 1922.
[2] *Ibid.*, pp. 60–63.

only common standard which all European countries could at present agree to adopt. . . . Successful maintenance [of the standard] would be materially promoted, not only by the proposed collaboration of central banks, but by an international Convention to be adopted at a suitable time. The purpose of the Convention would be to centralise and coordinate the demand for gold, and so to avoid those wide fluctuations in the purchasing power of gold, which might otherwise result from the simultaneous and competitive efforts of a number of countries to secure metallic reserves. The Convention should embody some means of economising the use of gold by maintaining reserves in the form of foreign balances, such, for example, as the gold exchange standard, or an international clearing system. . . .

When progress permits, certain of the participating countries will establish a free market in gold and thus become gold centres . . . : A participating country, in addition to any gold reserves held at home, may maintain in any other participating country reserves of approved assets in the form of bank balances, bills, short-terms securities or other suitable liquid resources . . . The ordinary practice of a participating country will be to buy and sell exchange on other participating countries within a prescribed fraction of parity, in exchange for its own currency on demand. . . . The Convention will thus be based on a gold exchange standard. The condition of continuing membership will be the maintenance of the national currency unit at the prescribed value. Failure in this respect will entail suspension of the right to hold the reserve balances of other participating countries. . . .

Each country will be responsible for the necessary legislative and other measures required to maintain the international value of its currency at par, and will be left entirely free to devise and apply the means, whether through regulation of credit by central banks or otherwise. . . . Credit will be regulated, not only with a view to maintaining the currencies at par with one another, but also with a view to preventing undue fluctuations in the purchasing power of gold. It is not contemplated, however, that the discretion of the central banks should be fettered by any definite rules for this purpose, but that their collaboration will have been assured in matters outside the province of participating countries. . . .

All artificial control of operations in exchange . . . should be abolished at the earliest possible date. . . .

The central banks concerned would agree to provide facilities for holding foreign balances (and securities) on deposit on account of other central banks, under special guarantees from each bank and from its Government as to the absolute liquidity and freedom of movement of such balances under all conditions, and their absolute exemption from taxation, forced loans and moratorium. . . .

Widespread Adoption of the Principle of the Gold-exchange Standard

For some years immediately following the report of the Genoa Conference, the principle of the gold-exchange standard in varying degrees was incorporated into the reconstructed monetary systems of most countries. The Bank for International Settlements[1] has tabulated the annual figures for the foreign-exchange holdings of European central banks for the period 1924 to 1932. Twenty-one of these banks had such holdings on the dates given for all 9 years, and three others had them for part of the time. The total amounts for the specific dates ranged from 12.9 billion French francs in 1928 to 2.9 billion in 1932.

[1] Bank for International Settlements, *The Gold Exchange Standard*, Annex I a.

The postwar gold-exchange standard rarely appeared, however, in anything like its pure form; and it was usually coupled, to a greater or less extent, with elements of the gold-bullion standard.

The Postwar Gold-exchange Standard Functioned through Central Banks. Unlike the prewar gold-exchange standard of the Orient, the standard after the war functioned largely through central banks of issue—a fact that necessarily brought about important changes in its character. In many countries, at least a specified minimum percentage of the legal reserve had to be kept in gold bullion and gold coin. This minimal percentage varied widely in different central banks. In other countries, any part or even all of the legal reserve, at the discretion of the central bank, could be kept in "foreign-exchange holdings." There were also great differences in the various countries as to the forms that these foreign-exchange holdings were permitted to take; *e.g.*, deposits in central banks and in the Bank for International Settlements, deposits in private banks, bank acceptances, trade acceptances, and short-time obligations of governments.

When under the prewar Philippine type of the gold-exchange standard a government sold for cash at home drafts on a reserve fund located abroad, it withdrew from circulation the purchase money and contracted the monetary circulation by the amount withdrawn; and when the foreign depository of the reserve sold drafts on the reserve fund in the home country, the draft was paid in cash, increasing the monetary circulation by its full amount. On the other hand, under the gold exchange standard of the later period when the agency within the home country that sold the draft on the reserve located abroad was a central bank of issue, and the funds received by it from the purchaser of the draft were bank funds, consisting chiefly of its own bank notes and of checks drawn by its member banks, no contraction of the currency was necessarily involved. The transaction was more in the nature of a transfer of credit, and the funds received by the central bank could be put back into circulation again at its discretion. On the other hand, the redemption of drafts drawn by the central bank's reserve agency abroad on the bank's reserve at home likewise did not of necessity involve any enduring expansion of the circulation at home.

It did not follow, therefore, under the postwar type of the gold-exchange standard that, when exchange rates rose to the gold-export point, registering a relative redundancy of the home currency, the redundancy would be removed by the sale of gold-reserve drafts; and that a decline of exchange rates to the gold-import point, registering a relative scarcity of money at home, would lead to an expansion of the currency in response to sales of drafts by the reserve agency abroad drawn on the reserve at home.

To meet this difficulty, some mechanism needed to be devised to bring about the required adjustments in the currency supply. The following method, with minor variations, was employed in many countries, including Chile, Colombia, Ecuador, Bolivia, and Peru. The example here cited is taken from the Peruvian central bank law of 1930.

In Peru the principal money of the country consisted of notes issued by the central bank, and the only central reserve used for maintaining the gold parity was that of the central bank. A large part of this reserve was kept in foreign financial centers, usually New York and London, in the form of bank deposits and of highly liquid short-time paper. The central bank obligated itself to sell drafts on a foreign depository, on demand, at the gold-export point, and provided for the sale of drafts by such a depository on the central bank at home, on demand, at the home gold-import point. These gold points marked the limits, as in the gold-coin standard, beyond which exchange was not permitted to go.

Under this system, in order to assure a contraction of the currency when sales of drafts at the gold-export point were depleting the gold reserves held abroad, the law provided that the central bank must pay a tax, the rate of which increased progressively as the bank's percentage of gold reserves declined below a certain specified point. The law provided also that the equivalent of this tax should be added to the central bank's discount rates. These requirements tended to enforce a contraction of the circulation when the currency was relatively redundant

[169]

and when, under the gold-coin standard, currency contraction would have been effected by gold exports. Under such requirements the central bank could expand its credit and increase its note circulation when its reserves were low and declining, *but only at a progressively increasing expense to the borrower and/or at a progressively declining rate of profit to itself.*

On the whole, and allowing for a few important exceptions, the postwar gold-exchange standard functioned successfully for several years, under principles laid down by the Genoa Conference, many of which had been widely adopted. Then, however, as the pressures that led to the world crisis beginning in 1928 to 1929 began to be felt, these principles were increasingly ignored, and gold-exchange stand-ards, like gold-bullion standards and gold-coin standards, broke down in the crisis and depression of the early thirties.

Weaknesses of the Postwar Gold-exchange Standard

Here one enters a technical and controversial field, in which only a few of the outstanding points need be considered in a study such as the present one.

The principal criticisms that have been made against the gold-exchange standard are the following:

1. *The Pyramiding of Gold Reserves.* Critics claimed that, in effecting an economy in the use of gold, the gold-exchange standard often carried too far the pyramiding of gold reserves. A computation, in a typical situation, of the "ultimate gold reserve

required to be held somewhere," under a gold-coin standard and the gold-exchange standard, respectively, for a country like Peru, showed 23 per cent for the gold-coin standard and 1½ per cent for the gold-exchange standard.[1] In some instances, the attenuation of these "foreign-exchange reserves," by way of pyramided credit, was much greater and, in extreme cases, it extended into rather "hot" money markets.[2] To help meet this difficulty, and at the same time enable the respective foreign central banks to keep informed regarding the volume of the exchange-reserve investments in the markets for which they are responsible, it would be good policy for central banks operating gold-exchange standards at home to conduct exchange-reserve operations abroad only with and through central banks and the Bank for International Settlements.

2. *Lack of Efficient Checks and Balances.* Another claim is that the gold-exchange standard does not automatically function so effectively, *i.e.*, set up as efficient a set of forces of checks and balances as does the gold-coin standard. Under the latter, one country exports gold at its gold-export point and another country receives the gold at its gold-import point. The monetary supply is contracted in the country exporting the gold and is expanded in the country importing it. Under a gold-exchange standard functioning through central banks at both ends of

---

[1] KEMMERER, in *Economic Essays in Honour of Gustav Cassel*, pp. 321–323.
[2] See Bank for International Settlements, *op. cit.*, pp. 18 and 19.

the line, drafts purchased at home, drawn on the reserve deposit abroad, are usually debited to a bank-deposit account at home and credited to one abroad; and the opposite takes place when a draft is sold by the reserve agent abroad on the central bank at home.

Such transactions normally would make no change in the amount of money in circulation within the home market or in the foreign ones. They would tend to decrease the volume of bank deposits in the country of the person buying the draft and to increase them in the country of the person receiving it. This, however, is a very different thing from the contraction and expansion of basic monetary gold in the respective countries. Ordinarily, a central bank through its loan, discount, investment, and exchange market policies is in position at will substantially to expand or contract its deposits, which are themselves the reserves of member banks.

The common statutory provisions for enforcing the desired currency contraction or expansion, at the gold points, through progressive taxes on reserve deficiencies and the passing on of these taxes to the public by adding their equivalent to the central bank's discount rate, were not wholly effective. In the first place, the "market might not be in the bank," and in the second place central banks were reluctant to pass the tax on to the borrower, since, if they absorbed it themselves, they could often take it out of profits that would otherwise be passed on to the government anyway in the form of a franchise tax or otherwise.

3. *Lack of Control by Authorities in the Home Country.* A group of further objections to the gold-exchange standard grows out of the fact that the gold reserves of a country are less in control of its own authorities when the reserves are deposited or otherwise invested abroad than when they are kept physically in the home country.[1] "If you have your gold at home . . . ," says Sir Otto Niemeyer,[2] "you can go to war with it." If the reserve is abroad, it may be seized by enemy countries in time of war, or it may suffer loss by the breakdown of the currency of the depository country as a result of war or other causes. Many gold-exchange standard countries suffered losses when England went off the gold standard in 1931.

4. *Effect on Public Confidence of Gold Imports and Exports.* Still another alleged weakness of the gold-exchange standard, as compared with the gold-coin standard, is psychological. There is a public awareness of gold exports and gold imports. In the market the influence of gold exports is "bearish" and that of gold imports is "bullish." Excessive gold exports weaken public confidence in the currency and lead to the hoarding of gold. These facts serve as checks against dangerous monetary and fiscal tendencies.

[1] In some cases of revolution, however, the reserve has proved to be safer abroad than at home.

[2] See, *The International Gold Problem*, p. 91.

When however, monetary adjustments are made, not by gold shipments, but by the purchase and sale of drafts at the gold points—something in which the general public has very little interest—these useful checks disappear. It is easier for the monetary authorities to take dangerous liberties with a gold-exchange standard than with a gold-coin standard.

The gold-exchange standard obviously has some decided merits, of which economy is the most important. It also has its shortcomings. The question of its future will be considered later.[1]

THE GOLD-BULLION STANDARD

Although gold in such unspecialized forms as dust, nuggets, bars, and the like, has been used as standard money for thousands of years, and although under the gold standard itself gold bars have been extensively employed in bank reserves and in making international payments, a formally and legally organized gold-bullion standard is an institution of comparatively recent development.[2] After the First World War, most countries returning to the gold standard adopted a gold-exchange standard, a gold-bullion standard, or a combination of the two.

Under a gold-bullion standard no national gold

---

[1] See pp. 209–222.

[2] As early as 1886 a gold-bullion standard was recommended for India by Lesley C. Probyn. The recommendation was repeated several times, with revisions of the plan, and was finally presented by Mr. Probyn in detail in his testimony before the Fowler Committee in 1898. See Fowler Committee, *op. cit.*, also, Kemmerer, *Modern Currency Reforms*, pp. 77–79.

coins are minted or circulated. The monetary unit consists of a fixed weight of gold, as in the gold-coin and the gold-exchange standards, but it is not coined. Gold reserves are held in the form of standard gold bars, mostly of large denominations, and the national currency is usually convertible into these bars on demand. The hoarding of gold is kept at a minimum, because the value of a gold bar is too great to make it easily available to the masses of the people.[1]

Aside from these differences, the fundamental principles under which the gold-bullion standard functions are the same as for the gold-coin standard and approximately the same as for the gold-exchange standard.

It is obviously easier, however, for a government to debase its monetary unit under a gold-bullion standard or a gold-exchange standard than under a gold-coin standard. This may be an important consideration for several reasons. (1) The masses of the people are not so much aware of a suspension of gold payments. (2) They have not in their power, through the privilege of ready redemption, the ability continually to bring pressure against inflationary trends. (3) Suspension of gold payment is easier for a government or a central bank to carry through if

---

[1] Of course, large bars may be cut up into small pieces by private individuals and sold to the public as merchandise, and this is done, to some extent. No gold is used in the form of coins for hand-to-hand circulation. The gold-bullion standard is, therefore, much more economical in its use of gold than is the gold-coin standard, although it is less economical than the gold-exchange standard.

it merely means a raising of the price of gold bullion or of gold drafts, than if it involves such vigorous action as the driving out of circulation and the outlawing of all the country's gold coins, as, for example, was done in the United States in 1933.

In the gold standard of the future the gold-bullion standard will probably play an important role.[1]

SELECTED BIBLIOGRAPHY

ARNDT, E. H. D.: *Banking and Currency Development in South Africa* (1652–1927), Juta & Co., Ltd., Cape Town, 1928.

Bank for International Settlements: *The Gold Exchange Standard*, a mimeographed manuscript, C.B. 60 Basle: B.I.S., 1932.

BROWN, WILLIAM ADAMS, JR.: *The International Gold Standard Reinterpreted*, 1914–1934, 2 vols., National Bureau of Economic Research, Inc., New York, 1940.

Commission on International Exchange: *Stability of International Trade*, Government Printing Office, Washington, D.C., 1903.

———: *Report on the Introduction of the Gold-exchange Standard*, Government Printing Office, Washington, D.C., 1904.

CONANT, CHARLES A.: The Gold-exchange Standard in the Light of Experience, *Economic Journal*, vol. XIX (1909).

Economic Essays in Honour of Gustav Cassel, George Allen & Unwin, Ltd., London, 1933.

Fowler Committee, Indian Currency Committee of 1898: *Report of the Committee Appointed to Inquire into the Indian Currency*, with *Minutes of Evidence* and *Appendices*, Eyre & Spottiswoode, London, 1890.

Genoa Conference: *Papers Relating to International Economic Conference, Genoa*, April–May, 1922, His Majesty's Stationery Office, London, 1924.

[1] See pp. 211–212.

KEMMERER, EDWIN WALTER: *Modern Currency Reforms* (with Bibliography), The Macmillan Company, New York, 1916.

————: The Establishment of the Gold-exchange Standard in the Philippines, *Quarterly Journal of Economics*, vol. XIX (1912).

————: A Gold Standard for the Straits Settlements, I and II, *Political Science Quarterly*, vol. XIX (1904) and vol. XXI (1906).

KEYNES, LORD JOHN MAYNARD: *Indian Currency and Finance*, Macmillan & Company, Ltd., London, 1913.

LINDSAY, A. M.: *Ricardo's Exchange Remedy*, Effingham Wilson and Co., London, 1892.

————: See Fowler Committee.

PROBYN, L. C.: *Indian Coinage and Currency*, Effingham Wilson & Co., London, 1897.

————: See Fowler Committee.

Royal Commission on Indian Finance and Currency: *Final and Interim Reports*, with *Minutes of Evidence* and *Appendices*, Eyre & Spottiswoode, London, 1913.

————: *Report, Minutes of Evidence* and *Appendices*, 3 vols., His Majesty's Stationery Office, London, 1926.

Royal Institute of International Affairs: *The International Gold Problem*, Oxford University Press, London, 1931.

CHAPTER VII

The Balance Sheet of the Gold Standard—Its Merits and Defects

Gold is tried with a touchstone, and men by gold.—CHILON, 560 B.C.

Up to this point our study of gold money and the gold standard has been concerned chiefly with history and fundamental principles. We have been looking at the past. Let us now turn to the future, and consider the principal merits and defects of the gold standard as a monetary standard for the postwar world—a very mundane sort of world, not Utopia.

MERITS OF THE GOLD STANDARD

Its Essentials Easily Understood

The first merit of the gold standard, as compared with other standards now competing with it for place in the monetary world, is its *simplicity*. In its essentials the gold standard is easily understood. The unit of value is a fixed quantity of a universally known commodity, which the people of the world, both primitive and advanced, have used as money for thousands of years. In a democracy it is highly important that the public shall understand their money. An old proverb says, "The people distrust what they do not understand." By this criterion, compare the gold standard with any of the numerous "price-index-number–managed-paper-money standards" now before the public.

High Public Confidence in Gold

Closely related to this merit of simplicity, is a second, that of *possessing the confidence of the public.* The instinct for gold is found among all peoples, savage and civilized, throughout history. Gold is today, as it has been for centuries, the most widely treasured and the most highly marketable commodity in the world. The familiar lines of Thomas Hood tell the story:

> Gold! Gold! Gold! Gold!
> Bright and yellow, hard and cold,
> Molten, graven, hammer'd, and roll'd;
> Heavy to get, and light to hold:
> Hoarded, barter'd, bought, and sold,
> Stolen, borrow'd, squander'd, doled:
> Spurn'd by the young, but hugg'd by the old
> To the very verge of the churchyard mould;
> Price of many a crime untold:
> Gold! Gold! Gold! Gold!
> Good or bad a thousand-fold!

The value of an ounce of gold, in terms of its purchasing power over commodities in the United States during the half decade 1936 to 1940, was greater than for any other quinquennium covered by our American price-index numbers dating back to 1801. This is true, moreover, despite the fact that the large world production of gold since 1929 is equal to the world's total known stock of monetary gold in 1923—the accumulation of the ages. No other kind of currency system in a distracted postwar world will so quickly restore the confidence of the public as a true gold standard. Can there be any question what the verdict would be, if you should put to a popular vote in the United States today the question: In what kind of dollar would you prefer to have your social security and your government bonds payable, a gold-standard dollar or a managed paper-money standard dollar? Gold does not need to be guaranteed. Everywhere it is accepted as final payment. Charles Dickens's phrase *as good as gold* means "the very best," the world over.

Its Highly Automatic Character, Calling for Little Political Management

The typical gold standard prior to 1914 was highly automatic. Gold flowed freely in international trade from the places where it was cheap to the places where it was dear, always seeking to maintain its international-value level, with free coinage in a large part of the world and with widespread interconvertibility on demand with other kinds of currency. Normally, man's interference with the automatic functioning of the gold standard prior to the First World War was small and was limited chiefly to the manipulation of discount rates by central banks and to a small amount of open-market operations.

[180]

The resort, moreover, to these means of "keeping under control" the international movement of gold frequently did more harm than good. The highly automatic character of the prewar gold standard was one of its great virtues. "We have gold," says an old proverb, "because we cannot trust Governments."

This distrust of government and politics in American monetary affairs has been deep and widespread for many years, and for very good reasons. Our record in this field has been bad, as have been the records of many other countries, notably those in Latin America and the Near East. Witness the blundering way in which our Congress handled American bimetallism from 1791 to the Civil War,[1] Jackson's war with the Second United States Bank, and our subsequent sad experiences with the bank notes of the wildcat banks. Witness our 17 years' experience with inconvertible greenbacks from 1862 to 1879, our unfortunate silver legislation of 1878 and 1890, and the absurd and highly expensive silver policies of Franklin D. Roosevelt's administrations.[2] Witness, further, the petition signed by 85 members of Congress in 1933 to President Roosevelt, asking him to appoint Father Coughlin as economic adviser to the United States delegates at the World Monetary and Economic Conference in London, and the subse-

[1] *Cf.* pp. 74–79.

[2] See CAROTHERS, NEIL, Silver—A Senate Racket, *North American Review*, January, 1932; also, *Kemmerer on Money*, pp. 122–140, and Kemmerer, *Money*, pp. 375–391.

[181]

quent jettisoning of that Conference by the President in the interest of the ill-fated Warren gold purchase plan. Witness the Thomas amendment of 1933, with its numerous monetary heresies, including the revival of long-discredited greenbackism.

With a record like this behind them, is it surprising that the American people have more confidence in a fundamentally automatic monetary system, that functions for the most part in accordance with nature's economic laws, than in highly managed systems that function chiefly according to the laws and judgment of politically conditioned men?

An International Standard

A fourth merit of the gold standard is its *international character*, a merit of great importance for the postwar period, when internationalism will be struggling for dominance over narrow nationalism.

Under the gold standard, although each country determines for itself the size of its monetary unit,[1] the standard itself in every country is gold. Prices are quoted in terms of gold and gold passes freely from country to country in making international payments. On the other hand, paper-money standards are essentially national or, at best, regional standards. Under them each country not only determines the size of its own unit of value, but also its own particular

---

[1] It is to be hoped that in the postwar decisions on this subject there will be friendly international counsel and cooperation. *Cf.* pp. 210, 212, 221 and 222.

standard of value, which, under most current plans, would consist of the value of a group of selected commodities, as that value was expressed in its own index numbers of commodity prices. These prices would of necessity be weighted according to the relative importance of the different commodities in each nation's own economic life. Both the commodities and the prices would be different for different countries, and so would be the methods of managing the standard and the successes or failures of the management. In this management, the monetary authorities would be continually subjected to political and fiscal pressures. All this means that managed paper-money standards would tend to become highly nationalistic standards. But such nationalism in monetary standards would bring into the functioning of international trade and finance many obstacles and much uncertainty.

In this connection, the present generation seems to be largely ignorant of the international monetary problems that most concerned its immediate predecessor. I mean those problems connected with trade and finance between countries on the gold standard and countries on other standards, such as the silver standard in China, India, and Mexico, and the paper-money standards of many Latin-American countries. The silver-standard countries presented serious problems, which were studied extensively by many financial commissions, practically all of which recommended as the only practical solution the replacement

[183]

of the silver standard by the gold standard, with the result that, prior to the First World War, the silver standard had practically disappeared from the world. China was the only important exception, and China herself then contemplated the early adoption of the gold standard. Similar difficulties forced numerous managed paper-money standard countries also to adopt a gold standard.[1]

The difficulties resulting from the existence of different standards in different countries—*e.g.*, the gold standard, the silver standard, and many different paper-money standards—were numerous; but the most serious of them related to trade and finance. Briefly stated, these difficulties were as follows.

Trade. When a country's currency depreciates in terms of the currency of other countries with which it carries on trade, the depreciation acts like a bounty on exports and a tariff on imports.[2] If, for example, it were the dollar that was depreciating in terms of the

[1] On the subject of the adoption of the gold standard by silver-standard countries, see the reports of the Herschell Committee and the Fowler Committee for India, those of the Mexican Currency Commission of 1903 to 1909 for Mexico, and the 1903 and 1904 reports of the United States Commission on International Exchange for these and other countries. These reports and other bibliographical material on the subject are listed in my *Modern Currency Reforms*, which is devoted largely to a study of replacing the silver standard by the gold standard.

I can speak with firsthand experience on the subject of the difficulties experienced by silver-standard and paper-money standard countries, since I acted as financial adviser to two silver-standard countries and 11 managed paper-money standard countries in the transformation of their currencies to a gold-standard basis.

[2] On this general subject see Edwin Walter Kemmerer, *Money*, pp. 142–153, and *Modern Currency Reforms*, pp. 488–494, and *passim*.

pound sterling, both commodity prices in the United States and the exchange rate in New York on London (*i.e.*, the dollar price of a pound sterling) would rise; but, since the exchange rate would be a much more sensitive price than the prices of most commodities, this rate would rise much faster than most commodity prices. This would mean that, while the American exporter to England would presumably be receiving the same sterling prices in England for his exports, he would be able to sell his sterling bills in New York for a continually increasing number of dollars to the pound, which would add proportionately to his profits and thereby stimulate exports to England.

On the other hand, this same depreciation of the dollar in terms of the pound would increase the cost of our imports from England. English prices would presumably be the same, while it would cost the importer in this country an ever-increasing number of American dollars to buy a pound sterling. Meanwhile, the prices of British goods would not have risen in the United States proportionately to the rise in the sterling exchange rate, so that the importer's profits would be reduced.

In the course of time, increasing exports from the United States to England and decreasing imports into the United States from England, with the corresponding price adjustments and gold movements, would restore equilibrium, and our inflationary bounty on exports and inflationary tariff on imports would disappear. They would, however, not disappear so long as the dollar should continue to depreciate in terms of sterling.

These artificially stimulated American exports would come into competition with the same or similar products in England and elsewhere abroad, where they would be looked upon as instances of "exchange dumping," and would cause resentment and fighting back in the form of countervailing duties and other trade restrictions. If the exchange dumping were carried far, it might well lead to competitive currency debasements.[1]

International Finance. Similar to the difficulties imposed upon international trade by nationalistic monetary standards, are the difficulties such standards impose on international finance both public and private.

If either the government or the people of a nation on one standard of money should borrow from a

---

[1] A striking example of how a depreciating monetary unit affects trade was cited many years ago by the British Consul General at Hakodate, Japan. "In 1892, Hakodate advertised for tenders for 1,500 tons of water-pipes and the contract was secured by a British firm, the tender being four guineas a ton. . . . At the price of silver four guineas cost Hakodate 28 silver dollars. In 1893 there came the greatest fall in the price of silver, the fall of last year [1908] only excepted. In 1894, Hakodate again advertised for 1,500 tons of pipes to complete her water system. The same English firm tendered, and this time at four sovereigns per ton. But because of the great fall in exchange it now required $40 [silver] to buy four sovereigns, or in other words, it required 40 per cent more of Hakodate's silver money to buy 5 per cent less of our gold money. Under these altered conditions Hakodate refused all the tenders; she erected her own iron works, and when last heard from was busy exporting her pipes to China and India."—Moreton Frewen, *Silver and Our Trade with Asia,* an address published by the Canadian Branch of the Fair Exchange League, P. O. Box 393, Ottawa, Canada.

country on another standard, with the debt payable principal and interest in the money of the creditor country, serious exchange risks would be involved. When the home country's money depreciates in terms of the money of the creditor country, whether it be on a gold, a silver, or a paper-money standard, prices, wages, and taxes do not rise proportionately to the rise in the debt charges.[1]

This is the principal reason why after the First World War there were so many defaults on international obligations. It was the principal reason, to take another type of example, why, a half century ago, British India decided to give up the silver standard and to go over to the gold standard. Every year India had heavy payments to make in England— the so-called *home charges*. These payments were on a gold basis; most of them were comparatively fixed. They covered such items as interest and annuities on the gold debt; salaries, pensions, and leave-of-absence allowances of British employees in the Indian service working in India or of employees who had returned to England from India and were there paid on a gold basis; purchases of supplies in England for the Indian service; and other expenses incurred for Indian governmental establishments. The total of these home charges for 1892 was computed at £16 million. Concerning the Indian financial situa-

[1] Of course, in the case of a depreciation of the creditor country's monetary unit, the opposite is the case. As a matter of fact, however, the currencies of debtor countries are much more likely to depreciate than are those of creditor countries. The debtor countries are usually weaker financially.

tion, Sir David Barbour, financial member of the Council of the Viceroy of India, in a public statement made in 1893 said[1]:

The immediate cause of our financial difficulties, and the cause which, by comparison and for the time being, dwarfs all others, is the fall in the gold value of silver, which . . . has added to the Indian expenditure in two years more than four crores[2] of rupees. . . . Our financial position for the coming year is at the mercy of exchange, and of those who have it in their power to affect in any way the price of silver. If we budget for the present deficit of Rx. 1,595,100, and exchange rises one penny [to the rupee], we shall have a surplus; if it falls a penny, we shall have a deficit of more than three crores; if we impose taxation to the extent of one and a half crores of rupees, a turn of the wheel may require us to impose further taxation of not less magnitude; another return, and we may find that no taxation at all was required.

Stability of Gold

Another advantage of the international gold standard is the stable value of gold, a subject previously discussed.[3] For the 94 years of the world's experience with an organized and full-fledged gold-coin standard, from the first adoption of such a standard by England in 1821 to its breakdown there in 1914 during the First World War, gold proved to be more stable in value than any other commodity.[4]

[1] Herschell Committee, *Report*, Section 5. (See Kemmerer, *Modern Currency Reforms*.)

[2] A crore is 10 million.

[3] See pp. 140–141.

[4] For a comparison with silver, see Kemmerer, *Money*, p. 375.

[188]

WHOLESALE PRICES IN ENGLAND DURING THE YEARS OF THE GOLD STANDARD[1]
(1913 = 100)

Year	Index number	Year	Index number	Year	Index number
1821	126	1855	119	1889	85
1822	123	1856	119	1890	85
1823	122	1857	124	1891	85
1824	114	1858	107	1892	80
1825	127	1859	111	1893	80
1826	111	1860	116	1894	74
1827	109	1861	115	1895	73
1828	105	1862	119	1896	72
1829	101	1863	121	1897	73
1830	100	1864	124	1898	75
1831	102	1865	119	1899	80
1832	101	1866	120	1900	88
1833	105	1867	118	1901	82
1834	105	1868	116	1902	81
1835	108	1869	115	1903	81
1836	121	1870	113	1904	82
1837	110	1871	118	1905	85
1838	112	1872	128	1906	91
1839	120	1873	131	1907	94
1840	116	1874	120	1908	86
1841	111	1875	113	1909	87
1842	101	1876	112	1910	92
1843	93	1877	111	1911	94
1844	94	1878	102	1912	100
1845	95	1879	98	1913	100
1846	95	1880	104	1914	100
1847	100	1881	100		
1848	91	1882	99	1925[2]	157
1849	86	1883	96	1926	148
1850	91	1884	89	1927	142
1851	88	1885	85	1928	140
1852	92	1886	81	1929	137
1853	112	1887	80	1930	120
1854	120	1888	82	1931[3]	103

[1] The period covered is 1821 to August 1, 1914, and April, 1925, to September, 1931.

[2] The gold standard was reestablished in April, 1925. Figures cover 9 months, April to December.

[3] The gold standard was suspended September 21, 1931. Figures cover 9 months, January to September.

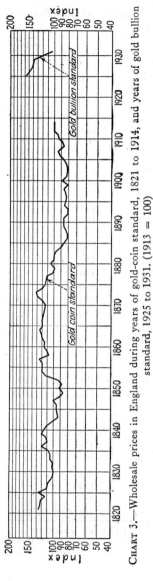

CHART 3.—Wholesale prices in England during years of gold-coin standard, 1821 to 1914, and years of gold bullion standard, 1925 to 1931. (1913 = 100)

The story of the value stability of gold as expressed in its purchasing power during the years of the gold standard in England and the United States is shown in the tables and charts on pages 189-194.[1]

For 19 of the 94 years ending in 1914 the British index number was between 95 and 105, and for 33 of them it stood between 90 and 110. For 5 different years (*viz.*, 1830, 1847, 1912, 1913, and 1914) it stood at 100. The range was from a high of 126 in 1821 to a low of 72 in 1896.

[1] For England the figures are those given by John Parke Young in *European Currency and Finance*, vol. I., p. 450, which were adjusted to a 1913 base. From 1821 to 1849 they were computed from the price data compiled by N. J. Silberling; and from 1850 to 1914 they are based on the Sauerbeck index numbers. Subsequent figures are those of the Board of Trade.

For the United States, the figures for wholesale prices are those of the Bureau of Labor Statistics adjusted to a 1913 base, and the figures for general prices (which cover wholesale prices, retail prices, security prices, and rents) are those compiled by the Federal Reserve Bank of New York.

In only 14 years of the 94 did the index number fall below 80 or rise above 120.

PRICES IN THE UNITED STATES DURING THE YEARS OF THE GOLD STANDARD, PRIOR TO ENTRY INTO THE FIRST WORLD WAR (1913 = 100)

Year	Wholesale prices	General prices[1]	Year	Wholesale prices	General prices[1]
1879	88	71	1899	75	74
1880	98	76	1900	80	76
1881	101	79	1901	79	77
1882	106	81	1902	84	79
1883	99	79	1903	85	80
1884	91	76	1904	86	81
1885	83	73	1905	86	82
1886	80	72	1906	89	85
1887	83	73	1907	93	89
1888	84	75	1908	90	89
1889	80	74	1909	97	93
1890	81	75	1910	101	96
1891	80	76	1911	93	96
1892	75	74	1912	99	99
1893	76	75	1913	100	100
1894	69	72	1914	98	100
1895	70	73	1915	100	103
1896	67	71	1916	122	117
1897	67	71	1917	165[2]	136[2]
1898	69	71			

[1] General prices cover commodity prices at wholesale, wage payments, elements of cost of living and rents. See Carl Snyder, A New Index of the General Price Level from 1875, *Journal of the American Statistical Association*, June, 1924.

[2] The United States virtually suspended the gold standard as of September 10, 1917, when the President's proclamation of September 7 became effective, placing rigid restrictions upon the exportation of gold. The figure here given for 1917, therefore, covers only the period from January through August.

During the 36 years of the prewar gold standard in the United States (1879 to 1914), the index number was between 95 and 105 for 8 years, and between 90 and 110 for 12 years. The range was from a high of 105 (in 1882) to a low of 69 (in 1874). In only 11 of the 36 years was the index number below 80.

Although this record of gold-standard prices covering nearly a century is far from a record of perfect stability, it is not a bad record. There is nothing that

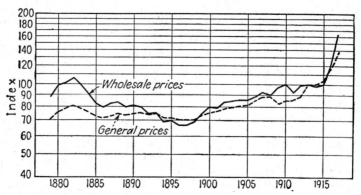

CHART 4.—Prices in the United States during the years of the gold standard prior to entry into the First World War. (1913 = 100)

remotely equals it, as far as I know, in any managed paper-money experience.

Lord Keynes, who in recent years has been one of the world's most vigorous critics of the gold standard, said in 1923, referring to England's experience with the gold standard during the nineteenth century and the early twentieth:

. . . the remarkable feature of this long period was the relative *stability* of the price level. Approximately the *same* level of price ruled in or about the years 1826, 1841, 1855, 1862, 1867, 1871, and 1915. Prices were also level in the years 1844, 1881,

[192]

and 1914. If we call the index number of these latter years 100, we find that for the period of close on a century from 1826

PRICES IN THE UNITED STATES DURING THE YEARS OF THE GOLD STANDARD[1]
AFTER THE FIRST WORLD WAR (1913 = 100[2])

Year	Wholesale price index number	General price index number	Year	Wholesale price index number	General price index number
1919[3]	206	173	1931	105	150
1920	221	193	1932	93	132
1921	140	163	1933[4]	87	129
1922	139	158	1934[5]	108	137
1923	144	165	1935	115	145
1924	141	166	1936	116	154
1925	148	170	1937[6]		
1926	143	171	1938[7]	112	154[8]
1927	137	171	1939	110	
1928	139	176	1940	113	
1929	137	179	1941	125	
1930	124	168	1942	142	
			1943	148	

[1] The term *gold standard* is used in the sense described on pages 134–138. The periods covered are from June 30, 1919, the date of the discontinuance of the wartime embargo on the exportation of gold, to March 6, 1933, the beginning of the nation's "bank holiday" under the President's proclamation of that date; and from January 30, 1934, the date when the Gold Reserve Act of 1934 became effective, to the present time (except for the period December 21, 1936, to April 14, 1938, when the government was sterilizing gold imports). See Kemmerer, *The A B C of the Federal Reserve System*, 11th ed., pp. 257–261.

[2] Figures have been converted to a 1913 base in order to make them easily comparable with those of the preceding two tables.

[3] For the period July to December.

[4] For the period January to February.

[5] For the period February to December.

[6] Not a gold-standard year, since the gold-import sterilization plan was in operation throughout the year.

[7] For the period May to December.

[8] This general price index number was not continued after 1938.

to the outbreak of war, the maximum fluctuation in either direction was 30 points, the index number never rising above 130 and never falling below 70. No wonder that we came to

believe in the stability of money contracts over a long period.
. . . [1]

Defects of the Gold Standard

The gold standard is far from being a perfect monetary standard. Although many of the charges brought against it by its opponents are either

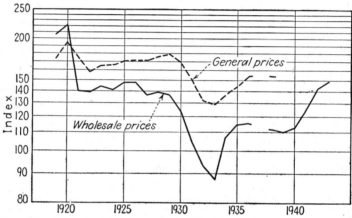

CHART 5.—Prices in the United States during the years of the gold standard after the First World War. (1913 = 100)

untenable or of little weight, some of them are important.

A Creature of Blind Natural Forces

The first defect is that under the gold standard, as under every other metallic standard, the value of the monetary unit is largely a creature of blind natural forces. As has been previously pointed out,[2]

[1] KEYNES, LORD JOHN MAYNARD, *A Tract on Monetary Reform*, pp. 11 and 12.

[2] See p. 139.

the unit is not a fixed value but the value of a fixed weight of gold, and this value is the resultant of the interaction of the forces of demand and supply. Whatever the future may bring forth, we must recognize that, down to the present time, man has not made much progress in bringing these forces under control. Gold production is carried •on by private enterprise in the quest of profit and without any conscious regard on the part of producers for the public's great monetary need of keeping the value of gold stable. The mines for substantial periods of time may pour large amounts of new gold on the market—as they did at the time of the California and Australian gold discoveries of the middle of the last century, and at the time of the great South African outpourings of gold for a couple of decades prior to the First World War—although the gold-standard nations of the world are suffering at the time from gold inflation. And the mines may be reducing their production of gold at times when these nations are suffering from gold deflation, as from the early seventies to the early nineties of the last century. In time, these evils correct themselves, but time is the essence and much hardship may be caused during the readjustment process. The public is, therefore, alternately in fear of a gold glut and of a gold famine.

Instability in Value

The second weakness of the gold standard—virtually a phase of the one just discussed—is the instability in the value of gold. In the interests of equity in relations between debtors and creditors and of a stable economy, the value of the monetary unit should not vary much from year to year or from decade to decade. But, as we have seen,[1] the value of gold does vary materially. A change in the purchasing power of the dollar in a given year, as in the United States in 1921, when it rose 10 per cent, or in 1937, when it fell 7 per cent, is serious; and more serious still is a continuous depreciation or appreciation over a period of years, as for the periods 1896 to 1910 and 1882 to 1886, respectively.

Rigidity

A third weakness, which is closely related to the two just mentioned but more questionable, is the rigidity of the unit of value. Under the gold standard, the unit of value cannot be easily changed as a means of adapting a national economy to the business cycle, to secular changes in the business world, and to the occasional violent disturbance. In order to obtain the advantages of a largely automatic monetary system and of stable foreign-exchange rates, a gold-standard nation must forego the privilege of manipulating its monetary unit to any considerable degree.

Expensiveness

Expensiveness is a fourth defect of the gold standard. In this connection, Adam Smith's statements are

[1] See pp. 89–91 and 188–194.

familiar.[1] Speaking of the use of bank notes as media of exchange, he said:

> The substitution of paper in the room of gold and silver money, replaces a very expensive instrument of commerce with one much less costly, and sometimes equally convenient. . . . The gold and silver money which circulates in any country may very properly be compared to a highway, which, while it circulates and carries to market all the grass and corn of the country, produces itself not a single pile of either. The judicious operations of banking, by producing, if I may be allowed so violent a metaphor, a sort of wagon way, through the air; enables the country to convert, as it were, a great part of its highways into good pastures and corn fields, and thereby to increase very considerably the annual produce of its land and labour.

The principal expense of a gold-standard currency may be measured by the interest, at the Government's long-time current rate, on the average amount of gold that the nation keeps in use for monetary purposes. At this writing (December 31, 1943), the United States' stock of monetary gold is, roughly, $22 billion—admittedly, much more than we now need. At 2½ per cent interest, the annual cost of this gold would be $550 million. Other costs incident to the gold standard are probably considerably less than they would be for a highly managed paper-money standard. Costs for abrasion, coinage, storage, and the necessary transportation in modern times are small, and the system itself being highly automatic calls for a minimum of managerial expense. The gold-

[1] SMITH, ADAM, *The Wealth of Nations*, Bk. II, pp. 292 and 325.

bullion and gold-exchange standards, as we have seen[1], are much less expensive than the gold-coin standard. On the other hand, the expenses of engraving and printing paper money, and of the high-quality paper itself that is required, calling as it does for frequent renewals by reason of wear and tear and obsolescence, and the higher cost of currency management, are substantial items in the cost of a managed paper-money system.

Essentially a Sterling Standard Prior to 1914

Another common criticism of the gold standard is that, although it worked well during the nineteenth century, while it was "essentially a sterling standard" controlled by one great central money market, London, it was unable to function after London lost her supremacy to New York following the First World War. Thereafter, London was a losing competitor with New York for first place, but, it was argued, the New York market had neither the organization nor the experience for taking over the new responsibility. Prior to 1914, New York's financial "hinterland" had been mainly the United States, while London's had been the world.[2]

By Way of Rejoinder

The replies that advocates of the gold standard would make to the criticisms just stated have already

[1] See pp. 160–161, 170–171 and 174–175.

[2] William Adams Brown makes much of this argument in his meticulous study *The International Gold Standard Reinterpreted.*

been made evident to a great extent to the reader, in previous discussions in this book. The rejoinders called for here, therefore, may be brief.

That the value of the monetary unit under the gold standard is controlled largely by blind natural forces and that it is not as stable as it ought to be are valid charges. Here the natural retort is the *ad hominem* argument. Managed paper-money standards are controlled by human forces of a volatile, emotional, and highly political character, and experience has shown that such standards, whatever they may have been in theory, have in fact been very unstable standards—much more unstable than the gold standard. It is unfair to condemn the gold standard of actual experience for not measuring up to a visionary's blueprint of a managed paper-money standard.[1] There is undoubtedly opportunity for improving both the gold standard and the various kinds of managed paper-money standards, by study, experimentation, and international cooperation. Experimentation, however, with a highly complex and delicate organism like money, which is enormously "affected with public welfare," is fraught with great danger. Public policy here should be a matter

[1] Elihu Root once said: "All my life people have been coming to me with plans to make over society and its institutions. Many of these plans have seemed to me good. Some of them have been excellent. All of them have had one fatal defect. They have assumed that human nature would behave in a certain way. If it would behave in that way almost any of these plans would work, but if human nature would behave in that way not any of the plans would be necessary, for in that case society and its institutions would naturally reform themselves to perfection."

of feeling one's way cautiously. This can best be done by starting from the time-tested gold standard.

In answer to the criticism that the gold standard is very rigid, the advocates of that standard say that this is more frequently a merit than a defect. It provides the monetary unit with a strong defense against fiscal and political exploitation. Managed paper-money standards are too pliable. They may not break, but how they can bend!

As to the argument that a gold standard is more expensive than a managed paper-money standard, the obvious reply is that a good monetary standard is so vital to the welfare of a nation that it justifies the payment of a good price, and that managed paper-money standards, *all things considered*, have usually in the end proved to be very expensive to the public. Furthermore, much can doubtless be done to make the gold standard of the future less expensive than was the usual gold-coin standard of the past.

As to the claim that the gold standard had become essentially a sterling standard and could not function after London lost its supremacy as the world's central money market, I believe that the distinction is one without a significant difference. The British gold standard was a true gold-coin standard down to 1914; after 1914 there was very little British gold standard, and that little was so weakly established as to be no reasonable guide for the future.

For generations prior to the First World War there was free coinage of gold in England, and English money of all kinds could be readily converted into gold at par by the public on demand. One could always change his bank notes for gold and his gold for bank notes. There was free and unlimited coinage of gold at the British mint, so that sovereigns could be obtained by anyone in unlimited quantities for gold bullion at any time at the mint or at the Bank of England, without appreciable charge; while gold coins could be transformed into gold bullion by the simple process of melting. There was a free market for gold within the country, and there were no restrictions on the exportation or importation of the yellow metal.

All kinds of money, therefore, were readily inter-convertible with gold coin and gold bullion on demand, and there was a free market for the gold. This meant that a £5 note could not be worth less nor more than 5 sovereigns, and that an ounce of standard gold in the form of sovereigns and an ounce in the form of bars could never differ appreciably in value. It, therefore, meant that changes in the world's value of gold communicated themselves quickly to British money. If a sovereign became worth appreciably more in England than its gold content of 113 grains of fine gold, gold bullion flowed to England and was coined into sovereigns, thereby increasing the supply of British gold coins; and if a full-weight sovereign in England became worth appreciably less than its pure-gold content of 113 grains, sovereigns were exported as bullion or melted down and transformed into gold bars for export or for merchandise uses, thereby decreasing the supply of gold coins in the British circulation.

This was the gold standard and it was also the "sterling standard." Fundamentally and viewed over any considerable length of time, they were the same thing. The short-time market, of course, was continually showing small aberrations from the norm— frictional points, as it were, in the functioning of the gold-standard machinery. Then, with the return to gold in 1925, the situation changed materially. The gold-coin standard gave place to the gold-bullion standard and there was much more monetary management.[1]

With the return to peace after the present war, the position of New York vis-à-vis London, in world financial affairs, will be relatively much stronger than

[1] There is "a myth widely current," says B. M. Anderson, that prior to 1914, "the world was on the sterling standard rather than the gold standard, that London controlled the gold standard and that it was only super-human wisdom in London which made it work. The doctrine adds that when New York became the center after 1918, the gold standard failed because New York lacked London's wisdom. Now the fact is that pre-war London had far less control and responsibility prior to 1914 than New York did after 1918, and that policy played a much smaller role in the earlier period. There were many gold standard money markets competing with London for gold prior to 1914, several of them very powerful, as New York, Berlin, and Paris, and many others of real influence, as Amsterdam, Vienna, Switzerland, the Scandinavian countries, and Japan. These all steadied one another. All would pull gold away from any country that was over-expanding credit, and force it to pull up. . . .

"I want to see a real gold standard world again, with several powerful money-centers competing for gold, and holding one another in check. . . . " *International Currency—Gold Versus Bancor or Unitas.* p. 16.

after the First World War. America will be much more international-minded than it was then; will be, relatively to England, in a stronger creditor position in the world's markets; and will have a banking system better organized for international business and provided with a much more experienced international banking personnel. The world will be a smaller world. If New York needs to take the leadership, she will be in a strong position to take it. We may hope, however, and expect that after the war there will be a much higher degree of international cooperation in monetary affairs than there has ever been before, and that this will be particularly true for the United States and the British Empire.

No Fair Test of the International Gold Standard Since 1914

The experiences of the world since 1914 throw very little light on the subject of the international gold standard. For this there are two reasons: (1) The world has had only a very limited experience with the international gold standard since 1914, and (2) nearly all the experience it has had has been with new forms of the gold standard established by financially weak governments in a very unstable postwar and wartime world.

The gold standard everywhere broke down during the First World War; and, with the exception of the United States, which returned to gold in 1918, there was no substantial return to gold until after the middle twenties. England did not return to gold until the summer of 1925, and did not complete her legislation for the return until July, 1928; Italy and Poland returned in 1927; and Sweden, in 1930. On this subject Brown says:[1] "In the history of the international gold standard 1928–1929 is a landmark because it was the only year during which that standard was almost universally in effect in countries not traditionally attached to silver." But, these were the years in which the world crisis began in Australia and Germany and Belgium.[2] It struck the United States in the stock-market crash of October, 1929, and soon led to the breakdown of all the recently established gold-standard systems of the world, those of Argentina, Austria, and Uruguay having broken as early as December, 1929.[3]

The Gold Standard in the United States, 1918 to 1933

The only important country having the gold standard throughout the decade of the twenties was the United States; and this country, after the great shock of the 1920 to 1921 postwar price adjustment[4] to gold, experienced for the 9 years, 1921 to 1929, one

[1] BROWN, WILLIAM ADAMS, JR., *The International Gold Standard Reinterpreted* 1914–1934, Vol. II, p. 773.

[2] See League of Nations, *The Course and Phases of the World Economic Depression*, p. 109.

[3] See pp. 120–121.

[4] From June, 1920, to June, 1921, wholesale prices in the United States fell 44 per cent, and general prices fell 19 per cent.

of the most stable *commodity price levels*[1] that the nation ever enjoyed. For these years our wholesale price-index numbers (on the 1926 base) were as follows:

1921	98	1925	103
1922	97	1926	100
1923	101	1927	95
1924	98	1928	97
		1929	95

There is no need of offering evidence in support of the second point, *viz.*, that the postwar gold standards established in most countries were weak types of the gold standard and were put into operation under very unfavorable financial conditions. These facts are everywhere recognized. Practically all these standards were gold-bullion and gold-exchange standards, as contrasted with the stronger gold-coin standard of prewar days. Nearly all the leading nations of the world had, financially speaking, been bled white by the war and found themselves under the necessity of resorting to rigid economy, high taxation, and extensive borrowing from abroad, notably from the United States. On returning to the gold basis, they perforce tried to get along with the minimum possible gold reserves, but the times were such that a restoration of confidence in the currency required higher reserves than under normal conditions. The temptation was great for governments to resort to monetary and credit inflation for fiscal

[1] During this period there were wide fluctuations in the prices of securities.

purposes. This policy, whenever extensively adopted —as it was widely—broke down the gold standard as it would have broken down any other stable money standard.

After the early thirties, the gold standard, for the second time in approximately a third of a century, was wiped off the map. It has been partially restored only in the United States and a few minor countries. The international gold standard has now for a number of years ceased to exist, and no useful conclusions concerning its merits or defects can be drawn either from America's present peculiar, nationalistic, administrative gold-bullion standard or from the pegged and unpegged managed paper-money standards existing elsewhere in the world.

SELECTED BIBLIOGRAPHY

ANDERSON, BENJAMIN M.: *International Currency—Gold Versus Bancor or Unitas*, Chamber of Commerce of the State of New York, New York, 1944.

BROWN, WILLIAM ADAMS, JR.: *The International Gold Standard Reinterpreted* 1914–1934. 2 vols., National Bureau of Economic Research, Inc., New York, 1940.

Cunliffe Committee: Committee on Currency and Foreign Exchanges, *First Interim Report*, His Majesty's Stationery Office, London, 1918.

————: Committee on Currency and Foreign Exchanges, *Report*, His Majesty's Stationery Office, London: 1918.

FISHER, IRVING: *The Purchasing Power of Money*, The Macmillan Company, New York, 1911.

————: *The Money Illusion*, Adelphi Company, New York; 1928.

————: Future of the Gold Standard, in John Parke Young's *European Currency and Finance*, vol. I, Government Printing Office, Washington, D.C., 1925.

GRAHAM, FRANK D., and CHARLES R. WHITTLESEY:*Golden Avalanche*, Princeton University Press, Princeton, N.J., 1939.

KEMMERER, EDWIN WALTER: Gold and the Gold Standard, *Proceedings of the American Philosophical Society*, vol. LXXI (1932).

————: *Our Present Gold Problem*, Hugh W. Long and Company, Jersey City, 1940.

————: *High Spots in the Case for a Return to the International Gold Standard*, The Economists' National Committee on Monetary Policy, New York, 1943.

————: *The A B C of the Federal Reserve System*, 11th ed., Princeton University Press, Princeton, N.J., 1938.

————: *Money—The Principles of Money and Their Exemplification in Outstanding Chapters of Monetary History*, The Macmillan Company, New York, 1935.

————: *Modern Currency Reforms* (with Bibliography), The Macmillan Company, New York, 1916.

KEYNES, LORD JOHN MAYNARD: *A Treatise on Money*, vol. II, The Applied Theory of Money, Harcourt, Brace and Company, New York, 1930.

————: *A Tract on Monetary Reform*, Macmillan & Company, Ltd., London, 1923.

————: *Essays in Persuasion*, Harcourt, Brace and Company, New York, 1930.

League of Nations: *Interim Report of the Gold Delegation of the Financial Committee*, Geneva, 1930.

————: *Second Interim Report*, Geneva, 1931.

————: *Report of the Gold Delegation of the Financial Committee*, Geneva, 1932.

Macmillan Committee: Committee on Finance and Industry, *Report*, and *Minutes of Evidence*, 3 vols., His Majesty's Stationery Office, London, 1931.

PALYI, MELCHIOR: *Monetary Chaos and Gold*, University of Chicago Press, Chicago, 1934.

Royal Institute of International Affairs: *The International Gold Problem*, Oxford University Press, London, 1931.

SPAHR, WALTER E.: *The Case for the Gold Standard*, Economists' National Committee on Monetary Policy, New York, 1940.

WHITTLESEY, CHARLES RAYMOND: *International Monetary Issues*, McGraw-Hill Book Company, Inc., New York, 1937.

YOUNG, JOHN PARKE: *European Currency and Finance*, vol. I, Government Printing Office, Washington, D.C., 1925.

CHAPTER VIII

The Monetary Standard of the Future

The future is purchased by the present.—SAMUEL JOHNSON.

Concerning the world's monetary standard of the future the logical conclusion to be drawn from the preceding discussion may well be summarized in the following excerpt from the 1931 report of the Macmillan Committee, which consisted of 14 eminent British financiers and economists:

There is, perhaps, no more important object in the field of human technique than that the world as a whole should achieve a sound and scientific monetary system. But there can be little or no hope of progress at an early date for the monetary system of the world as a whole, except as the result of a process of evolution starting from the historic gold standard.

With what sort of a gold standard should the world begin its postwar monetary economy? That is a large question, and all that we may hope to do by way of giving it an answer within the limits of one chapter of a small book is to state briefly a few general principles.

PRELIMINARIES

By way of preliminaries, six principles should be followed. They are these:

[209]

1. The subject is an international one, and its satisfactory solution demands a high degree of international cooperation, which should begin at once and continue indefinitely. It should include small nations as well as large ones. There is no place for stabilization competition such as the world experienced after the First World War, when a number of countries resorted to monetary-unit undervaluation, in the effort to improve their competitive position vis-à-vis other countries in the export trade.

2. The monetary unit should be established in each country after conference with other countries, but without any compulsion whatever from them. The determination of the size of a nation's monetary unit is affected with such a great public interest and so highly prized as a prerogative of sovereignty that it is impracticable to subject it to outside interference. The new unit should be approximately the value of the monetary unit in operation at the time the stabilization is effected, or some easy multiple of that unit.

3. Inflationary policies should be discontinued at the earliest possible date after the armistice, and everything possible should be done by the government to inspire confidence in the currency.

4. Measures providing for the ultimate discontinuance of all artificial price and exchange controls should be taken early, but the process of discontinuing them should be put into effect by cautiously measured steps.

5. After prices have settled down to what, for want of a better name, may be called their *natural level*, there should be a tryout *de facto* stabilization of the monetary unit at this level.

6. The *de facto* stabilization in due time should be followed by a *de jure* stabilization, but the latter should not be adopted until the government is in a strong enough position financially to be confident that it can make such a stabilization stick.

TYPES OF POSTWAR GOLD STANDARD

As has been previously noted, there are three important types of gold standard, *viz.*, the gold-coin standard, the gold-bullion standard, and the gold-exchange standard. These types frequently overlap, and each of them is found in many varieties. Each type has its own advantages and disadvantages, and these are relative to the economic, fiscal, and political conditions in the different countries. One type is best adapted to one country and another type to another country. The gold-coin standard is the strongest type domestically and puts up the best defenses against disturbances from abroad. On the other hand, since it provides gold coin for internal circulation and makes it easily accessible to hoarders, the gold-coin standard is the most expensive type in the amount of gold it requires.

The gold-exchange standard, on the other hand, while requiring gold or gold credit only for exchange purposes at the limits marked by the gold points, and while keeping this gold abroad, normally for the most part in the form of bank deposits, is the least expensive. The gold-bullion standard provides no gold for internal circulation and makes it difficult to obtain gold for hoarding. Its reserves, however, are held in the form of gold bullion. Therefore, although requiring less gold than the gold-coin standard, the gold-bullion standard requires much more than does the gold-exchange standard. Consequently, it takes an intermediate position. In general, the richest nations would probably choose the gold-coin standard, while the poorest nations, as well as colonies and other dependencies, would prefer the gold-exchange standard. Countries in an intermediate position would prefer the gold-bullion standard.

The shifting from one type of gold standard to another might be used as an instrument of international monetary policy directed toward the stabilizing of the value of gold. If, for example, a situation should develop in which gold production was falling off and the world's supply of monetary gold was lagging behind the world's demand, it would be desirable to economize the use of gold. This would dictate shifts from the gold-coin standard to the gold-bullion and gold-exchange standards. If, on the other hand, gold production should increase unduly, with a resulting tendency to gold inflation, there could be shifts in the opposite direction—*i.e.*, toward the gold-coin standard—so as to increase the demand for gold.

IMPLEMENTATION OF INTERNATIONAL
GOLD STANDARD

A popular idea, but a fallacious one, is that metallic-money standards, like the gold standard, are entirely automatic in their operation, and that paper-money standards are entirely managed and not automatic at all. All monetary standards in modern times are more or less managed. It is not a question of the presence or the absence of monetary management, but rather of the extent and character of that management. With the gold standard, the management that will be required should be imposed upon a monetary system that is fundamentally automatic in its functioning and should be conducted according to certain established principles that will be accepted by the world's leading central banks under the authority of their respective governments. With reference to this management or nonmanagement, the following general principles should be followed.

There should be no restrictions on the holding by the public of gold coin or gold bullion within the country or on the free coinage of bullion at the mints or the melting down of gold coin. The exportation and importation of gold should be free from all trade restrictions and tariffs. Under such conditions, gold will enjoy a very high degree of fluidity in its movements both national and international, and the value of the gold monetary unit in each gold-standard country will be held very close to that of its gold equivalent in every other gold-standard country and to the value of gold bullion in the free markets of the world.

There should be a high degree of freedom in the international movement of goods and services. The gold standard can function over high tariff barriers, as it has many times in the past, but high tariff barriers are obstacles to international trade and finance and to the smooth and orderly functioning of any monetary standard.

On this subject there has been much confusion growing out of the popular notion that gold moves in international trade only "to pay balances." As a matter of fact, gold moves for the same fundamental reason that any other commodity moves—to seek the best market. It goes abroad whenever it is worth abroad more than it is worth at home, by a sufficient margin to yield an attractive profit after paying all the expenses of its exportation. Its importation from abroad is merely the other side of the same shield.

As a general proposition, omitting such things as gifts and losses by shipwreck, bankruptcy, fraud, and theft, a nation's total exports—visible and invisible—are equal to its total imports—visible and invisible—when viewed over a substantial period of time. If this were not true, a nation would either be getting goods from abroad free or giving away goods to foreigners. If, for example, a country is normally exporting 50 different commodities and services (including gold, from time to time) and is normally importing 60 different commodities and services (including gold, from time to time), the 50 commodities on the one side and the 60 on the other will be in balance. The balance will be destroyed if *any* commodity on either side is omitted, and this is no more true of the commodity gold than of any other commodity in the balance sheet. Gold normally moves very easily in international trade, because it is the most marketable of all commodities. It does not move "to pay a balance," in any true sense of that term.

A country that has sold goods in a foreign market has a credit there that it can draw upon for the purchase of any goods for sale in that market at the current market price, and this applies as fully to gold as to any other commodity. Viscount Goschen once said, in speaking of England's position,[1] "Our powers of obtaining gold would only be exhausted when the country had nothing left to sell."

Henry Thornton, at the time of the famous Bullion Controversy in England early in the last century, said concerning the place of specie in international trade:[2]

Our ancestors, eager for the acquisition of the precious metals, exploring, as is well known, new continents, chiefly with a view to this article; and accustomed to consider trade as profitable or otherwise, in proportion as it brought in or took

[1] GOSCHEN, GEORGE JOACHIM, VISCOUNT, *Essays on Economic Questions*, p. 68.

[2] Henry Thornton in Hansard, vol. XX, pp. 81–85, 1811.

out gold and silver, were naturally led to denominate that part of our exports or imports which consisted of these metals, a balance. In truth, however, this was not a balance. Bullion was an article of commerce, rising or falling in value according to the supply and the demand, exactly like any other, transporting itself in greater or less quantities according to the supply and the demand, exactly like any other, transporting itself in greater or less quantities according to the comparative state of the market for that and for other articles, and forming only an item on one side of the general account. Corn, or any other commodity, might just as properly be said to pay the balance as gold or silver; but it would evidently be inaccurate to affirm that corn discharged it, because it would imply that the amount of all the articles except corn was fixed; and that these having first adjusted themselves with relation only to each other, a given quantity of corn was then added to pay the difference. It was, for the same reason, inaccurate to affirm, that gold or silver paid the difference.

Continuing this argument later, he said:

Suppose a fisherman on our southern coast, to collect a thousand guineas, and exchange them in the channel with some French fisherman for as much French brandy as should be deemed an equivalent, the gold, according to the doctrine in fashion, would have gone to pay the balance of trade. It would have been employed to discharge a previously existing national debt. It was always, according to these tenets, the brandy which forced out the gold, and not at all the gold which forced in the brandy. By the Frenchman's putting the brandy into his boat, the Englishman was compelled to put the gold into his. The brandy always went before; the gold always followed after. It was one of the peculiar properties of gold that it always served to pay a balance.

GOLD CONVERTIBILITY

There should be interconvertibility on demand of all kinds of nongold money with gold coin, gold bars, or gold drafts, as the case may be.

Such interconvertibility serves the gold standard in three different but closely related ways.

1. It keeps all the different kinds of money—*viz.*, gold coins, notes, fiduciary silver coins, and minor coins—at a parity with each other. It does so through providing the machinery by which excessive issues of any particular kind of money are promptly withdrawn from circulation and deficiencies in the circulation of any particular kind of money are made up.

2. The convertibility into gold on demand, by creating confidence in the currency, increases its acceptability by the public in times of low public confidence and thereby checks "flights from the dollar" and the resulting enlargement of the currency supply, which would otherwise be caused by the increasing velocities of circulation.[1]

[1] A good example of the way changes in the public's confidence may, by influencing the velocities of circulation, affect the monetary supply and thereby the value of the money, is found in the experiences of Germany following the First World War.

In 1922 and 1923 the German people's confidence in the mark declined very rapidly, there was a "flight from the mark into goods," and the velocities at which mark currency circulated increased enormously, with corresponding increases in commodity prices. In 1922, according to Schacht, "The rush to get rid of cash as soon as possible . . . led to an extraordinary increase

3. The third function that convertibility performs is fundamentally the most important one. It is the function of maintaining the gold parity of the monetary unit by continually adjusting the currency supply to the changing currency demand. In this connection, a nation's gold reserve functions as a buffer fund or, as it is sometimes called in Spanish, a *funda reguladora*. The process may be briefly described as follows.

When, under a normally functioning international gold standard, the supply of currency in any country becomes excessive relative to the demand, as compared with other countries, money becomes cheap at home relative to abroad, prices of commodities and of securities tend upward, the exchange rates move toward the gold-export point; and, when that point is reached, gold is sufficiently more valuable abroad than at home to make its exportation profitable. The exportation of gold is an evidence that, under

---

in the rapidity of the circulation of money. Everyone who had payments to make, endeavored to make them as quickly as possible, before he could be caught by the depreciation." In the autumn of 1923, the Rentenbank law was passed, which made the old reichsmarks convertible into a newly issued and well-secured rentenmark at the rate of on trillion to one, and which gave the rentenmark a gold value of approximately 24 cents United States money. The conditions of the stabilization were such as to give the public confidence in the new money, and greatly to decrease the "flight from the mark," thereby reducing the velocity of mark circulation. This reduction was so great at the start that it resulted in an actual scarcity of money and the German authorities were compelled to increase the volume of paper money in circulation in order to maintain the approximate price level prevailing at the time of the stabilization. See Hjalmar Schacht, *The Stabilization of the Mark*, pp. 68–69; also, Edwin Walter Kemmerer, *Money*, pp. 287–289.

existing conditions of business, there is a relative redundancy of currency circulation at home. Since local paper money and fiduciary coins have almost no international market, the redundant currency is drained off largely in the form of gold exports. These exports are continued until the exchange rate falls below the gold-export point and the currency supply is reduced to a quantity that places the price level of a country more nearly in equilibrium with the price levels of other countries, or, in other words, until the reduction of the country's money supply has made the monetary unit so valuable at home that further exportation of gold becomes unprofitable.[1]

Under conditions of such currency redundancy and resulting gold exportation, the central banks must always be in a position to give out gold freely for exportation, as long as it is required, to relieve the country of its relatively redundant currency and to force exchange rates below the gold-export point, thereby bringing the country's price level and dis count rates back more nearly into equilibrium with those of the rest of the world.

Obviously, a country's normal gold reserve should be sufficient to provide for the absorption, through redemption in gold, of any currency in circulation that may be rendered excessive by the usual fluctuations in business. In addition, it should be large enough to afford a reasonable margin of safety for extraordinary emergencies.

---

[1] *Cf.* KEMMERER, *op. cit.*, pp. 136–140.

The Gold Standard and the Central Bank

The principal monetary authority in each country should be a central bank. On this subject the recommendation of the Brussels International Conference of 1920 was sound in saying that " . . . in countries where there is no central bank of issue, one should be established. . . . " In the interest of an efficient administration of the gold standard, the central bank should have the exclusive right of note issue, and the gold reserve of the nation should be centralized in the bank. The central bank should be controlled by a board of directors on which there should be representatives of the government, representatives of the member banks, and representatives of business, as is the situation in many South American countries, including Chile, Colombia, and Peru. No single group should preponderate.

While no one denies that a nation's central bank should be administered with primary regard to the public welfare and with very little effort to earn profits above a modest return on capital, it is not so well recognized that, in the great majority of cases where central banks have suspended gold payments, this has been done under the political pressure of governments to meet fiscal needs. The trouble has been caused much oftener by governmental exploitation than by exploitation for profit by private interests. Gold reserves have been unduly depleted, not so much through being drawn out of the country by

foreign countries as through being flooded out by
fiscal inflation at home. The nation's monetary
authority, which should be the board of directors of
the central bank, should have a substantial government representation but should not be under government domination. This is the very realistic lesson of
monetary history.

An International Bank

An efficient international gold standard will call
for an international bank, with which the central
banks of all gold-standard countries should be
affiliated and to which they should contribute the
necessary capital.

The functions of this bank should be exclusively
of a monetary and banking character. It should be a
central bank of central banks. It should not make
long-time loans to its member banks or otherwise
enter the field of fiscal operations. Such activities
may be very important in international affairs, but
they belong to agencies other than the international
central bank.

The principal functions of the bank should be (1)
to serve as an international clearinghouse for the
member central banks; (2) to hold part of the reserves
of the member central banks; (3) to collect, organize,
and help interpret for its members international
credit, monetary, and other financial information;
(4) to serve as a meeting place for conferences both

formal and informal of member bank officials—a function that the existing Bank for International Settlements has usefully performed.[1]

INTERNATIONAL MONETARY CONFERENCE

Finally, the United States government should promptly declare its intention to rehabilitate its own gold standard after the war, and should call an international monetary conference of all countries desiring to return to a gold basis, with the object of formulating plans for the restoration of the international gold standard and for international cooperation to make that standard a better standard.

SELECTED BIBLIOGRAPHY

Bank for International Settlements: *Annual Reports*, Basle.

CASSEL, GUSTAV: *Money and Foreign Exchange after* 1914, The Macmillan Company, New York, 1922.

DEKOCK, M. H.: World Monetary policy after the Present War, *The South African Journal of Economics*, June, 1941.

DULLES, E. L.: *Bank for International Settlements at Work*, The Macmillan Company, New York, 1932.

The Economist: The Future of Gold, *The Economist* (London), 1942.

EINZIG, PAUL: *The Bank for International Settlements*, Macmillan & Company, Ltd., London, 1930.

GIDEONSE, HARRY D.: *The International Bank*, Rutgers University Press, New Brunswick, N.J., 1930.

GREGORY, T. E.: *The Gold Standard and Its Future*, E. P. Dutton & Company, Inc., New York, 1931.

[1] See DULLES, E. L., *Bank for International Settlement at Work*, pp. 460–461, and 476–478.

HAWTREY, R. G.: *Monetary Reconstruction*, 2d ed., Longmans, Green and Company, London, 1926.

———: *The Art of Central Banking*, Longmans, Green and Company, New York, 1933.

———: *The Gold Standard in Theory and Practice*, Longmans, Green and Company, New York, 1927.

KEMMERER, EDWIN WALTER: *High Spots in the Case for a Return to the International Gold Standard*, The Economists' National Committee on Monetary Policy, New York, 1943.

———: *Modern Currency Reforms*, The Macmillan Company, New York, 1916.

———: *Money*, The Macmillan Company, New York, 1935.

Kemmerer Commission: *Colombia, Leyes Financieras Present-adas al Gobierno de Colombia por la mision de expertos los años de 1923 y 1930 y exposicion de motivas de éstas*, Editorial de Cromos, Bogota, 1931.

———: *Chile, Commission of Financial Advisers, Monetary Bill and Bill Founding the Central Bank of Chile* (with reports in support thereof), Government of Chile, Santiago, 1925.

———: *Poland, Reports Submitted by the Commission of the American Financial Experts*, Ministry of Finance, Warsaw, 1926.

———: *China, Commission of Financial Experts, Project of Law for the Gradual Introduction of a Gold Standard System in China* (together with a report in support thereof), Shanghai, 1929.

KEYNES, LORD JOHN MAYNARD: *A Tract on Monetary Reform*, Macmillan & Company, Ltd., London, 1923.

KJELLSTROM, ERIK T. H.: *Managed Money*, Columbia University Press, New York, 1934.

League of Nations: *The Course and Phases of the World Economic Depression*, Secretariat of the League of Nations, Geneva, 1931.

LEHFELDT, R. A.: *Controlling the Output of Gold*, the Author, London, 1926.

MLYNARSKI, FELIKS: *Gold and Central Banks*, The Macmillan Company, New York, 1929.

PASVOLSKY, LEO: *Current Monetary Issues*, Brookings Institution, Washington, D.C., 1933.

REDELMEIER, W.: *The Gold Standard*, The MacLean Publishing Co., Ltd., Toronto, 1941.

SCHACHT, HJALMAR: *The Stabilization of the Mark*, George Allen & Unwin, Ltd., London, 1927.

SPAHR, WALTER E.: *The Case for the Gold Standard*, The Economists' National Committee on Monetary Policy, New York, 1940.

YOUNG, JOHN PARKE, Editor: *European Currency and Finance*, vol. I., Government Printing Office, Washington, D.C., 1925.

Index

A

America, discovery of gold in, early nineteenth century, 74–76
middle of nineteenth century, 77–80
Anderson, B. M., 202
Angel, gold coin of early England, 33
Aristophanes, principle of Gresham's law mentioned by, 9
Arndt, E. H. D., 152
Arts, gold in, 147–148
As, weights and varieties of, in early Roman times, 11–15
As libralis, 11–13
Asia Minor, coinage of, in ancient times, 5–7
Assyria, early coins of, 6
Augustus, Caesar, 18
Aureus, of Constantine, 19–21
divisions of, 17
of Julius Caesar, 18–19
weight of, reduced in early Roman times, 18–19

Australia, discovery of gold in, 80
effects of, on value of gold, 195
Austria, stabilization of money in, following First World War, 112
Austria-Hungary, adopts gold-exchange standard, 153
Automatic nature of gold standard, 180–182

B

Bank checks, extent of use in U.S. in 1914, 104
Bank-deposit and bank-note currency in U.S., 1896 to 1914, 101
Bank holiday of 1933 in U.S., results of, 122–126, 193
Bank for International Settlements, 166–167, 171
Bank notes in U.S., circulation of fractional parts of, about 1850, 81
depreciation of, in 1813, 47

Wilbur, Ray Lyman, 123
Windom, William, 95
World Economic Conference of 1933, 128, 181, 182
World supply of gold, 20, 122, 195
World War, First, effect of, on gold standard, 108–120

Y

Yellowbacks (gold certificates), 102–103
Young, John Parke, 190

Z

Zecchino, Venetian gold coin of Middle Ages, 21